THUG LIFE

SETH FERRANTI

HAMILCAR
PUBLICATIONS
Boston

THE
TRUE
STORY
OF
HIP-HOP
AND
ORGANIZED
CRIME

ISBN: 978-1949590-51-7

www.hamilcarpubs.com

Aut viam inveniam aut faciam

To all the hustlers, players, OGs, gangsters, gangbangers, thugs, and solid motherfuckers who I did time with in the Bureau of Prisons for twenty-one years. From 1993 until 2015 the BOP was my home and I met a bunch of real, thorough, and vicious dudes. This book is for all of you. You know who you are.

Contents

Intro

I STARTED WRITING ABOUT GANGSTERS IN PRISON while doing a twenty-five-year sentence in the feds for a drug conspiracy. You always hear about writers taking stuff out of context and misquoting people, but in prison there was no room for that. If I misquoted someone in there, I would have gotten six inches of steel in my back. I wrote within the "Death Before Dishonor" code and I learned that those who came up at the intersection of hip-hop and organized crime lived by this code. It wasn't a catchphrase; it was a way of life. Most of the people I cover in this book epitomize that code. They were the guys calling the shots, the gun thugs, the gangstas, the movers and shakers.

The streets are cutthroat, dog-eat-dog, and coming up in that world isn't easy, but in the parlance of the street, *the drug game became the rap game*. It was a natural evolution. That *get mine or be mine* mentality that defined the streets shaped the world of hip-hop. The only problem was that some dudes had trouble leaving the streets behind. Once you start getting that fast money, it's not easy to give it up.

Young Black men who moved from the streets to hip-hop found a way out of the trap, but many were targeted by law enforcement because of the color of their skin and what they represented. That's the real point of these stories. As the denizens of the block fought their way to legitimacy, they were being scrutinized because of their race. The systemic injustice that has occurred when a person of color becomes successful goes against what this country is supposed to stand for. Coming up from nothing is part of the American dream.

But the white establishment and law enforcement don't want to believe that a Black man has gone all the way legit. If they rap about it, they must still be doing it. But, as this book shows, that's not always the case. There's a fine line between reality and fiction when it comes to rappers. Just look at how many cases have been recorded in the annals of hip-hop lore. These men who made it should be celebrated, not persecuted.

But it's a fact that for all those who made it, just as many fell by the wayside and ended up with life in prison or worse. Just look at Tupac and Biggie. Death and prison are always in the cards when you're a Black man in America, despite your success. That said, I hope you enjoy these stories for entertainment purposes, but I also hope they help you see the larger picture. I wrote this book to cement these men's legacies in the chronicles of pop culture and gangsterdom, but also to show the reality of the American dream, and who it is or isn't truly meant for.

PART 1

1980s

*Back in the
Day*

THE CRACK KING OAK

Too Short
and
Daryl Reed

1

AT THE END OF 1988, JUST AS TOO SHORT was getting ready to record his classic album, *Life Is . . . Too Short*, Darryl "Lil D" Reed was charged in federal court with conspiracy to distribute sixty-eight pounds of crack cocaine. The Alameda County deputy district attorney, Russ Giuntini, called Reed "the most feared drug dealer in Oakland." And Oakland narcotics officer Ken Scott claimed that Reed "rose from street dealer to multimillionaire." But sometimes there's more to the story than the mainstream papers and the feds tell you.

Two years before Lil D was arrested, Congress passed the Anti-Drug Abuse Act of 1986, a law that targeted African Americans who were using and selling crack cocaine. Crack cocaine was punished a hundred times more severely than powder cocaine, creating a 100:1 ratio that pushed systemic racism. Guys from the inner-city all across the nation were getting their heads cracked and being sent to prison for disproportionate terms. Five grams of crack triggered a mandatory-minimum sentence of five years in prison. Not to say that Lil D was a small dealer. He was far from it, but the feds were actively targeting Blacks and trumping up charges. The feds claimed the drugs seized were worth three million dollars. They wanted to bury Lil D.

"Lil D bust was one of the DEA's biggest busts in U.S. history in Oakland," said "Shakim Bio Chemical" (aka John Edwards), the incarcerated author of *The Last Illest* and whose life allegedly inspired Oliver "Power" Grant's character "Knowledge" in the film *Belly*. Imprisoned for almost thirty years, Shakim Bio, a Queens native and former street general, is well respected in both the federal and Ohio state systems—not only for being a go-hard prison gangster, but for his knowledge of hip-hop and crack-era lore and the streets. He is the type of dude the term *Original Gangster* was intended for.

"In 1988, [Lil D] had the biggest birthday party at the Golden Gate Fields Turf Club," Bio said. "He had like 3,500 guests, all partying and breaking bread with the young twenty-year-old kingpin. Lil D was definitely the youngest in charge and had major fame in Oakland's streets. The feds ran up in one of his spots, got him with like multiple kilos of crack and powder."

Bio added: "Lil D was the type who didn't mind getting his hands dirty. He was that type of boss. Had millions of dollars' worth of work in the crib, getting it rocked up himself. One of them hating-ass snitches done put the peoples on D. He got thirty-five years in the feds for manufacturing and possession of crack to sell. He still lived like a king in prison and made shit happen."

Lil D was known to be a key part of the hip-hop scene in Oakland. Before he got locked up, he served as a mentor to up-and-coming rappers and took a big interest in the burgeoning industry. He was the connection between the streets and the rap world, a man who would make things happen by supporting his peers who were creating a worldwide phenomenon with their music, style, and words. In the early days of hip-hop, the rappers looked up to the street dudes. These were the guys who they were emulating and whose style they were copping.

"When hip-hop first came out our way, it attracted everyone from all over; no matter what you were into at that time, it was something new and different, very relatable," said Dan "Hands," a fifty-seven-year-old convict from Oakland, California, who's been in the federal system for twenty-two years and is currently incarcerated at USP (United States Penitentiary) Atwater, a vicious penitentiary where *take it to the wall* is the mentality.

He continued: "It's something that was ours. Listening to these early songs by Sugar Hill, Grandmaster Flash and the Furious Five, Melle Mel, Kool Moe Dee, Run-DMC, LL Cool J. . . . [There are] too many to name, but you can see that I do know my shit. Anyway, we also started writing our own versions and creating our own styles in the Bay Area."

Known throughout the federal system as "Hands" because of his ability and proclivity for knocking motherfuckers out, the Oakland native is older now and doesn't move the same, but, even so, he's managed to maintain the stellar reputation that says everything in the belly of the beast. He's been at Atwater for twelve years now, after doing ten years in the penitentiaries back east, and he's known as the type of cat who doesn't take any shorts. It's *get mine or be mine* for the Bay Area gangster.

"Yeah, I'm from Oakland, California, born and raised," Hands said. "Ask about me. I was robbing everything, anywhere there was money at, Dan Hands was there too. I hit everything from shopping malls, department stores to drug dealers, gambling spots, bar none. That's what I'm in for." In the hood everything goes, and some dudes are known for putting that crazy strong-arm game down.

Hustlers come in all forms and fashions, and the street legends who held sway in the crack era were gangsters of the highest order—triple-A bona fide. Dudes who were about getting theirs and holding down the neighborhood. Not to say that it's all good, because crime is crime and violence is violence, but the way the legends carried it made them a little different. At least in the annals of gangster hip-hop lore.

"Daryl Reed, who was known as 'Lil D,' was that dude," said Dan Hands. "He was getting a lot of money in Oakland and other cities, known and unknown. It ain't my job to speak on that. They didn't call him 'Lil D' cause he was a little dude. Nah, he was a young old cat, a cat before his time. The way he thought and operated, like some West Coast New Jack City shit in the '80s. He was heavy in the streets and gave back plenty to the community."

Lil D had blood uncles who ran with the 69 Mob, but he was primarily exposed to the drug game as a twelve-year-old child through underworld icon Felix "The Cat" Mitchell. Because of their closeness, street lore held that Mitchell was his "uncle," but in reality, he was a loose relation. Felix Mitchell had a child, Felix Wayne, with Lil D's aunt. But he took a shine to the young hustler and took him under his wing, giving game, and mentoring the up-and-coming gangster in his own way.

"At the time Felix Mitchell was the biggest heroin drug kingpin," explained Lil D in an interview with VladTV. "Felix and them had they operation going on in Oakland so I was exposed to that environment by spending a lot of time over at my grandmother's house in the projects. . . . Being in them Rolls-Royces, man, and watching this fly guy with all these beautiful women. He was like Robin Hood to us, you know. He had an influence on me. Even though my parents tried to keep me away from that and shelter me, it was kind of impossible because I was spending so much time in the projects."

Lil D's mobster uncles and surrogate uncle Felix Mitchell taught the eager youth the rules of the drug game, grooming him and making him aware of not only the wealth that came from dealing but also the potential dangers if you slipped up. When Lil D looked at how they were living, driving around in Rolls-Royces while his working-class parents struggled to make ends meet, he decided street life was more exciting and lucrative. He started out in the game by doing simple favors for the gangsters such as going to the store for them in exchange for a little cash in his pocket. These simple errands led to doing things such as holding their guns (as the police would be less likely to search a child).

Lil D invested the money Felix gave him into buying marijuana. As a fourteen-year-old, he assembled a crew and had four to five older guys on the block selling for him. This led to even more money that he stockpiled in secret so his parents wouldn't find out. When they asked where he got his money to buy things like clothes, Lil D told them he had a hustle scalping tickets—which was partially true. Even at a young age Lil D was a true hustler who looked for any angle to make money—whether legal or illegal. It's just the nature of the game.

As crack hit the streets, the youngster was surprised to find out that little white rocks were bringing twenty bucks apiece. Lil D spent $160 for a sixteenth of cocaine, which was converted to crack and given to a friend to sell. "He came back to me in a couple hours and he told me it was gone. I couldn't believe this. I came up there and I saw these people lined up to get these little rocks," recalled Lil D. "Within a month and a half, we started making so much money from these rocks I didn't want to sell marijuana anymore. . . . I loved math. I was doing numbers in my head and said, 'I'm gonna be a millionaire.'" Soon after, he was getting up to $15,000 a day as a high school student; Lil D was well on the way to that first million. A hood entrepreneur in the truest sense.

Hands said that when Oakland rappers Too Short and MC Hammer needed a way, Lil D was their way. "He made it happen for them. He was like what Harry O was to Suge Knight. Lil D was that guy to both Too Short and MC Hammer. Supporting them and helping them out financially when they were just beginning and trying to establish themselves in the rap game." The street dudes loved the rappers because the rappers captured the lives they were living in verse.

According to Lil D, he hired MC Hammer to play his birthday party. The two established a lifelong friendship, and Hammer would later write the introduction to Lil D's autobiography. Too Short had a hustle making mixtapes and for twenty dollars he would name-drop the street gangsters in his raps. Lil D often bought several copies to pass out to his crew. If they were going to be bumping music, it had to be shouting out the name Lil D loud for the streets to hear.

With the respect of Lil D came serious financial backing. While the up-and-coming hip-hop stars like Too Short and Hammer made albums, shot videos, hit the stage, and began gaining an audience, Lil D was the power broker behind the scenes. The gangster invested heavily, forming companies and paying for studio time, music-video production, and tour buses. He was funding his culture and way of life.

Shakim Bio: "Just because you come from the neighborhoods these rappers rap about doesn't mean that they were involved in the activities of these neighborhoods. Some of these rappers are just what they are—rappers. That still doesn't take away from their ability or their talent, but some needed the push of those who were a part of the hood activities to get [their] talents noticed."

When rappers started forming their raps, their style, they spoke about what they saw, what they witnessed in the streets. Hands said, "They were telling the stories of the hood, same way you be reading those hood novels now. They were verbally and poetically doing that in the '80s. Only a gifted muthafucka can do that, use words to paint a story." It was art imitating life in full swing.

With these stories, the lyricists became "hood reporters," chronicling the attitudes, style, and challenges of street life. At first the audiences were small and fans were from these same neighborhoods. Later, when hip-hop began getting national radio play, the rappers gained a much wider audience and the potential to make lots of money. For many, the music business was seen as an opportunity to get out of the hood and escape a cycle of poverty. But attracting the attention of neighborhood peers and recording industry executives were two separate things.

In a time before social media, a rapper had to make a loud enough noise to be heard in the offices of the record companies. Like any business, making money requires spending money, a challenge for individuals coming up in areas plagued by poverty. Making the jump from performing on porches and in parks to venues and stadiums often required the interest and support of hustlers who had the means and money to help them in their rise to stardom. Drug dealers like Lil D funded the hip-hop movement and in turn made it what it is today.

Dan Hands: "Even basketball players in the hood, they were like unsigned rappers, they needed to take steps to be seen too. That's where the hustler comes in. Behind every success story in the hood is a story of one who was involved in crime. He was the one who financially backed up the play of how things got to be noticed. It comes from that hustler who not only took a chance, but believed in the person with the talent."

Too Short was born Todd Anthony Shaw on April 28, 1966, in Los Angeles, California, but in the early '80s his family moved to Oakland. He was a drummer in the band during his high school years. A pioneer of West Coast rap, Too Short began rapping in 1983. In the mid-'80s, along with high-school friend Freddie B, Too Short started making rap songs on cassette tapes that circulated in Oakland and the Bay Area.

"Back then, rapping wasn't no hustle for no hustler. It was music they listened to and enjoyed, but hustlers couldn't do what rappers do—put those stories together," Hands said. "Hustlers wished they could rap. Back then rappers was telling the stories of the hustlers and life itself— that's what made the hustlers want to get involved. That was who Daryl 'Lil D' Reed was. He was that one true hustler who believed in dudes and took chances to change lives."

In 1985, Too Short released his debut album *Don't Stop Rappin'* as a solo artist on Oakland label 75 Girls Records and Tapes. Shortly after, Too Short and Freddie B formed the label Dangerous Music to distribute their albums regionally and then they formed the rap group The Dangerous Crew with others.

Dan Hands: "Too Short is not only a rapper who raps, he raps that pimp shit; that's his art. Like you got rappers who spit in certain categories: the gangsta rapper, the conscious rapper, the comedian rapper, ladies'-man-love-song rapper. Too Short talks that certified pimp shit, that's his lane."

Dangerous Music became Short Records and then changed to Up All Nite Records, but Too Short didn't sign a major deal until 1987, with Jive Records, which released his album *Born to Mack*. In 1989, Too Short followed up with the iconic classic and career defining *Life Is . . . Too Short*, which drew worldwide acclaim with the hit-single title track. Too Short is recognized as one of the first hip-hop artists to use the word "bitch" in his music, and it would become one of his trademarks.

Hands: "He is so into that life. I know one time when I was in USP Edgefield in S.C., when it was a pen—yeah, it was a pen first before they turnt it to [an] FCI medium—I was there in 2001 to 2003. There was this pimp from ATL who was pimping hard, feds locked him up for pimping, his name was Scooby or some shit like that. He talked about fucking with Too Short on that pimp shit. Showed me some photos with Too Short."

Since the release of the *Life Is . . . Too Short* album, the rapper remained prominent in the hip-hop industry for over thirty years. From 1987 to 2020 he released over twenty-two albums. Too Short also did some work in the adult film industry and was instrumental in the invention of the "hyphy" music movement that emerged out of his home base of Oakland that he used to put the spotlight back on local artists.

"Too Short was well known all over the globe and shit, but heavy in ATL. Scooby got 'Pimp of the Year' and 'Mack of the Year' awards. Big trophies and shit. In those photos Scooby [showed] me The Bishop Don Juan and Too Short was the ones presenting him with the trophies. That's how serious Too Short is about pimping. He makes pimp music. You remember that song 'The Ghetto'? That came out in 1990? That song was hot. My nephews said that shit was in the *Grand Theft Auto: San Andreas* video game. Now how about that shit?"

MC Hammer or simply Hammer, born Stanley Kirk Burrell on March 30, 1962, was known as a commercial rapper, record producer, performer, and entrepreneur, and had been recognized worldwide for his ability to dance his ass off in shiny pants. During the late '80s to the early '90s Hammer killed the music scene with "U Can't Touch This" and "2 Legit 2 Quit," becoming a megastar in the process. Hammer was also known for the intricate choreography he taught his Oaktown's 357 girl rap group and his dancing entourage. He even challenged Michael Jackson to a dancing contest and started a trend with those baggy Hammer pants.

Dan Hands: "You see once MC Hammer got really, really, really on he tried to give back and look out for everyone he could think of. From the hood to the police force. He wanted to do what Lil D did. Hammer damn near went broke."

Both rappers made huge contributions to hip-hop culture. Both started trends that generated millions and millions of dollars—for their record companies and distribution companies as well as themselves. Their lives changed and they changed many lives with their investments and businesses inside and outside the culture of hip-hop, but in reality, none of it would have ever happened without the assistance of Lil D.

Hands: "Lil D was once called the Crack King of Oakland. He had the whole city on lock. East, West, and North Oakland. He was the man and showed love everywhere he went. He did so much for people that there was a golden rule—don't fuck with Lil D. You knew better than to rob or touch anything that was his or connected to him or his."

He added: "President Obama gave him a pardon in 2016 and he came home in 2017 after doing twenty-six years out of thirty-five. The city welcomed him home and you know they took care of him. Real legend right there. All he got to do now is kick his feet up. Hip-hop is going to take care of him. But I'm sure he has something big planned, don't be surprised."

Even while incarcerated, Lil D told his story to give kids the benefit of his experience, urging them to stay away from drugs and violence. Lil D would call into radio stations and worked with the Urban Peace Movement and Silence the Violence to promote a positive message to his communities. He even wrote *Weight,* a book about his life. Lil D was one of 774 people who were granted clemency by President Obama at the end of his term.

Shakim Bio: "President Obama was trying to right the wrongs of the War on Drugs. He saw how it was unfair and sentenced African Americans disproportionately. I think it was a good move. . . . Especially the nonviolent offenders like Lil D who served almost three decades for the same drug amounts as white and Spanish cocaine dealers who got out in ten."

In an interview with *Complex,* Lil D gave his thoughts on the sentencing disparity he was forced to endure. "I didn't get thirty-five years because of drugs; I got thirty-five years because of the powers that be. It was bigger than just me. And the bigger plan was to incarcerate the African American male," Lil D said. The 100:1 crack cocaine sentencing disparity has since been changed to 18:1 and there's been some talk of making it 1:1, but until that happens, the system of racial injustice will remain.

THE DIRTY
SOUTH
HOU

Rap A Lot
cords and
Prince

2

A LOT OF PEOPLE DON'T KNOW THAT THE CEO and owner of Rap-A-Lot Records came from Houston's notorious Fifth Ward, where he was hustling drugs and stacking money all through the early '80s at the height of the crack era. Like any other inner-city kid coming of age in the capitalistic and materialistic '80s, when life was cheap and you gained respect at the point of a gun, it wasn't easy to level up, especially legitimately. It was strictly by any means necessary.

Growing up in the infamous Coke apartments in the Fifth Ward, otherwise known as the "Bloody Nickel," J Prince overcame tremendous obstacles to not only survive but thrive. He has always been a man of few words, but when this Houston OG talks, people definitely listen. He put Texas rap on the map and has always been considered the fourth member of the Geto Boys, one of the pioneers of gangsta rap.

J Prince, born James L. Smith on October 31, 1965, was tired of living that dangerous lifestyle, where you can't trust anyone, not even your own family. He'd paid a dear price, losing family and close friends to drugs and the inevitable violence that comes when you play the game. He knew there was a better way. You can't really enjoy that lifestyle when you never know what to expect.

In this world, future superstars who were hustling on the come up had to dodge the traps of the thugs and stickup kids around them who were trying to take it all away. With every rise in the street game came the chance of a fall. Because while you were stacking your money, someone else was plotting to take it. One bad decision and everything you worked for could evaporate in an instant.

The Fifth Ward was like any poor hood in America: a clusterfuck of gun thugs, pimps, hustlers, con men, prostitutes, crack dealers, roughnecks, sneak thieves, gangsters, and gold diggers. Urban communities filled with public housing projects and low-income neighborhoods, polluted with drugs and high crime, where death and murder around every corner were the norm—a vortex of tragedy, heartbreak, and lost lives. But J Prince rose above his surroundings. He was on a mission.

"Through trial and error I was able to figure out things rather quickly," J Prince told NPR in 2012. "When you're from the hood, when you're from a situation where sharks swim around you every twenty-four hours, then it's almost a part of your character to figure out how to survive. This was something that I was used to."

"I grew up where poverty was a serious burden on my family and that had a major part in my mind developing," J Prince said. "I wanted to break that poverty curse that existed. Even as a kid I was somewhat abnormal for my age when it came to trying to have a dollar. I was seven or eight years old and a lot of [other kids] were thinking about playing, but I was thinking about how to get a dollar, whether it was through cutting yards or whatever."

His early hustles were creative. He stole a pony and charged neighborhood kids to ride it. When *Pac-Man* came out, he rented an arcade cabinet and kept it in his backyard shed for kids to play. It was the top-selling machine in Texas. J Prince interned at a bank as part of a high school work program, only to find himself laid off. From that point on he vowed to work only for himself. He hit the street. But you can only go so far hustling drugs, even though a lot of youngsters in the hood don't know that.

By the age of twenty-one, J Prince had saved $100,000 from his street hustles. He used it to realize a dream he'd shared with his dead sister. As children they had wanted to buy their mother a house and vacuum cleaner. J Prince did both. "Money. Ahhhh, it felt good not being broke," J Prince wrote in his autobiography *The Art and Science of Respect*. "I was addicted to the feeling of freedom. I loved the fact that I was improving my financial state every day. I became the provider in my mother's house. I retired her. It was an honor for me to be able to provide for someone who had provided for me all my life."

But with money came paranoia—and a feeling that the street life was going to catch up with him. "My hardened soul was thawing and every part of me felt on fire. I knew I'd crossed too many lines. I had enemies in the streets, waiting to see weakness in me," he wrote in his autobiography, "I felt myself being watched. I knew they were looking for my vulnerabilities. Many of my friends were dying, being hunted down in the streets like animals. I was sure my phone was tapped, which usually means the feds are listening. If they're listening, a case is coming." Such feelings would make their way into the lyrics of "My Mind Is Playin' Tricks on Me" by the Geto Boys.

The only peace that J Prince could find during this dark period was in the recording studio working with a group he was calling the "Ghetto Boys." It was there that he could breathe and forget his fears. In the studio he thought realistically about his future in the streets. Some people can't do that. They get greedy, and comfortable taking dangerous chances. It becomes a way of life. Quitting his hustles and putting his savings into the rap game would be a downgrade and involve a pay cut. But as J Prince put it, "It'd be a step down from being *the man*, but being *the man* came with a heavy price."

When J Prince became a father, he knew he had new responsibilities. Few of his friends had their fathers around growing up. He wanted to see his kids grow up to be successful. He wanted to teach them to do right and see them graduate from school. He knew it had to start with him, so he made a decision.

"It was more of a reaction from other people. It was the beginning of me planting a seed for my brother," J Prince told *Complex* in 2011. "His name was Sir Rap-A-Lot. And then there were a couple guys, Raheem and Jukebox, skipping school. So I made a deal with them—y'all go to school, I'll support you in rap. They put me in a position where I had to honor my word because every day after school they would show up at my grandmother's house and be performing on the porch."

His word was important to him, and J Prince promised himself that he would give up hustling drugs and put the same energy into being a successful businessman in legal activities. He knew that if he wanted to make money in America, he had to be a business owner. It was all about ownership. He had enough sense that he could see working for someone else was a sucker's game.

"I think it had a lot to do with Fifth Ward, our hood," Prince told NPR. "We were only holding a mirror up to things that we had lived through in our surroundings, which are the same [things] that exist in ghettos around the world. So it was easy for people to embrace our subject matter."

J Prince started as a party promoter. That was his first idea to make money. He had connections and knew a lot of people from the dope game, and he intended to use those relationships to his advantage. He saw the future and placed all his bets on a culture and genre that his people created—hip-hop. He just had to find out how to become a part of it.

In the neighborhoods where J Prince and his friends grew up, people could relate to the struggles that hip-hop talked about. The music attracted people who were caught up in the same struggles. It reflected the ghettos of America. A visual scene depicted in words. Raw and honest.

"The roots are very deep." J Prince told *Complex*. "I always enjoy being a quiet storm. I like to make a lot of moves and not create a lot of noise in the process of making them. You had Def Jam, Run-DMC, and all those guys out that way. That was basically it. Then you had Ice T, he was the only other guy that was on the scene from the West Coast at the time."

It was the 1984 Fresh Fest tour that attracted J Prince to promote shows. He was always the one who wanted to be the behind-the-scenes type of person who made things happen. He had the mind of an entrepreneur and still carried that hustling DIY spirit. He just wasn't into perpetrating illegal moves to get to it anymore; it was hard work or nothing. He saw what was happening in the hip-hop world and just had to translate that energy to Texas.

"I had to figure out a way to circumvent them monopolizing the South the way they was doing," Prince told NPR. "We figured that out and a lot of times it wasn't always pretty—but the results were fruitful, and that's the reason the South is so dominant today. It's because of the trails that we blazed way back then."

J Prince started Rap-A-Lot Records in 1987 and for over thirty-five years has worked to promote Houston's rap scene and rap artists. And when it comes to business, he's worn every hat—music executive, promoter, CEO, producer, and even boxing manager. Rap-A-Lot Records was first distributed by A&M Records with the release of Raheem's 1988 debut, *The Vigilante*.

The label was distributed through the '90s by EMI's Priority Records (1991–1994), Noo Trybe Records (1994–1998), and Virgin Records

(1998–2002). In the early 2000s the company was distributed by Asylum Records and then Fontana Distribution. In August of 2013, Rap-A-Lot announced a distribution deal with RED Distribution.

Prince told *Complex*: "When I first started Rap-A-Lot, maybe the first year or two, I wasn't as involved as I should have been. I was doing other work. You know, I was making money doing other work. And it was with my last piece of money that I decided to get involved and do everything my way. That record for the world, globally, was "Mind Playing Tricks". Now, before "Mind Playing Tricks", the one to really get us a lot of street credibility was Scarface's "The Dope Game Cocaine". And that's the song, from a street perspective, because we didn't get radio or video with that song, but it was huge. It was huge enough to take us gold, just off of that one song. It was so strong; it was a street anthem."

J Prince was the inspiration and motivation that got Master P's No Limit Records to follow his blueprint. Known artists of his Rap-A-Lot Records were the Geto Boys, Devin the Dude, Do or Die, UGK (Pimp C and Bun B), Scarface, Yukmouth, Big Mike, YBN Nahmir, and HoneyKomb Brazy. Prince even tried his hand and succeeded in the boxing game, managing Floyd Mayweather, Andre Ward, and current star Shakur Stevenson among others.

"Boxing was my first love before hip-hop, really. I was inspired by Don King," J Prince said. "I used to watch him all the time as a kid and I used to wonder about this man's hair that stuck up straight like that. I wanted to tap into the boxing world, and I got distracted by the hip-hop thing, which was a good distraction for me."

Prince continued: "But eventually I was able to, after being attacked by the feds and all them different people, I had to show them that I wasn't one-dimensional, to the extent where I diversified my portfolio into the boxing arena. But the overall business, [there's] a lot of resemblance there. First of all, when you're dealing with a rapper and boxer, both of these guys is from my hood. You know what I'm saying? These are my people. I grew up with both of them."

It took a while before the New York rap scene would give their respect to J Prince and Rap-A-Lot, but they came around as he forged connections on the East Coast. Jay Z said, "When you do business with [J Prince], you're held at your word. You know if he tells you something, he's gonna do it, which is refreshing." Music exec Lyor Cohen said, "J Prince knows exactly and precisely what he wants to accomplish, and he sets his mind out to accomplish it." A man of honor in the rap game that just wasn't about stunting.

J Prince to *Complex*: "I consider myself a lion. You know what I'm saying? It's a lot of my younger brothers that look up to me that I want to inspire. I know I've inspired a lot of them, from Master P to Cash Money to Tony Draper, and a gang of others that I don't know about. By me keeping my independence and showing that I can survive in the midst of it."

Even with his success, he was well acquainted with being under investigation and scrutiny by the FBI, DEA, ATF, IRS, and local law enforcement. They were upset that they couldn't get him in the '80s and, now that he was legit, they felt he didn't deserve to be on top. J Prince had built up a whole community and they were still aiming to trap him off. All these elements worked together to make him a legend in the Dirty South. As a successful Black man, he was a target.

For almost a decade, beginning in 1988, Houston narcotics officers and the DEA targeted Prince and Rap-A-Lot-Records by infiltrating Houston's Fifth Ward with the goal of getting a conviction against him. Over twenty arrests were made during this time—with charges ranging from murder to drug use to drug sales—but no proof was ever established that Prince was guilty of any crimes. The feds usually determine who they want to arrest in an investigation before even investigating. They rely mostly on cooperator testimony and shape the narrative to their agenda.

The DEA began attempting to groom informants in the Fifth Ward to implicate J Prince, who they wanted to take down under the RICO Act. "The only way that we were going to get the target [James Prince] of this investigation was through a conspiracy," DEA Agent Howard said. The DEA was willing to do almost anything to make the case that the label was a front for a major trafficking network. They even made rapper Scarface a target of the probe, hoping they could flip him.

"In regards to the U.S. Attorney's Office, we could not convince them to indict Brad Jordan, aka Scarface, even though I strongly believe we had him tied in solidly on a federal drug-conspiracy charge," said James B. Nims, a Group Supervisor in the DEA. "This was devastating to the case as we felt that Brad Jordan could have provided us with important leads and information regarding Mr. Smith [J Prince]."

J Prince saw it all in a different light. "Here's what I believe with all of my heart. I'm a guy that made a transition from the streets to corporate in my early twenties," Prince told Joe Rogan in December 2020. "We were considering starting a Black-owned distribution [company], 'cause we felt like it was a need for an artist coming after us, and we wanted to make a better way and a smoother way for them. Because even back then they wasn't gonna allow any more Master Ps, Cash Money, Irv Gottis, independents. I was like . . . let me counter, and make another avenue for the youth to come in after us."

Despite all this J Prince just kept doing what he did, working to promote underprivileged neighborhoods and communities. He was helping to rebuild them by building churches, recreational centers, schools, and boxing complexes. He was doing all in his power to better the communities. In January of 2007, Houston's mayor Bill White and the City Council honored Prince for his more than twenty years of commitment and dedication to the city. J Prince was a hero to his city and to his world.

Despite the accolades, J Prince keeps it humble. "I was blessed to be able to give back to these and others who contributed to my life in some significant way. Now I'm in a position to take care of them because they took care of me," he wrote in his autobiography. "That's the ultimate high for me; I don't even need drugs. There's no better joy to me, than to become a blessing to a person who contributed to my journey."

J Prince is an OG who maintains respect because he always remained true to his roots and presented nothing fake. He put Houston on the hip-hop map with Rap-A-Lot and let the world know there were others making noise outside of the East and West Coasts. He hit big with the Geto Boys and then put Drake on. He even maintains that he was the one to tell drug lord Michael "Harry-O" Harris to connect with Dr. Dre, the first step in a process that would lead to Death Row Records. J Prince is simply a beast. Wherever he is at, he'll go down as the one making power moves behind the scenes while always giving back to those around him.

THE ORIGINAL GANGSTA LA

Ruthless Record and Eazy-E

3

THIS IS THE STORY OF A HUSTLER who ran the streets of Compton, California, at a time when gang violence was leaving dead bodies everywhere. When the crack era was raging and in full effect. When gangs were a national scourge and made headlines every day. The young Black male was vilified in the media, and for brothers in the hood, life was either cut short by a barrage of bullets or a lengthy prison sentence. It was an ugly era in America's history.

Much has been made of Eazy-E's gangster past, but it was his entrepreneurial mind and spirit that built a blueprint with N.W.A. and Ruthless Records that set trends and showed others the way to do this rap thing. Eazy-E blazed the path and hip-hop culture followed. Gangsta rap was born and West Coast hip-hop went mainstream. Eazy-E left a legacy that will always be remembered in the annals and lyrical lore of hip-hop and gangsta rap.

"Yeah, he was a little hustler," Ice Cube told *Rolling Stone* in 1991, referring to his first impression of Eazy-E. "You know, his shit was just all fresh and clean, little jewelry on. You could just tell what somebody was doing. I admired him, you know. He was making money in the neighborhood, you know what I'm saying? He had money, he had his clientele, he was doing his shit, didn't ask nobody for shit, so yeah, I dug him."

Eric "Eazy-E" Wright was born September 7, 1964, in Compton, California. While the city today has a notorious reputation for crime and violence, in the '40s and '50s it was a middle-class mecca for families relocating after World War II. At the time, racial discrimination and fierce segregation led to a divide between East Compton and West Compton. East Compton remained primarily white and was briefly the home of future-President George Bush in 1949.

Meanwhile, West Compton saw a postwar migration of Black families from the south. Part of this was because of its geographical location near Watts, which had a growing Black population as well. With spacious single-family houses and good neighborhoods, Compton was seen as an attractive location to escape the poverty of the agricultural south and raise a family. But as Black families moved in, white flight began to take place to neighboring communities that remained racially exclusive, a phenomenon that accelerated when the Watts riots brought violence in 1965.

Eric was born just one year before the nearby Watts Rebellion, which involved thirty-four thousand people and the destruction of a thousand buildings with property damage of $40 million. The infamous incident was one of several urban riots that signaled a time of racial unrest and an increase in violence in what had once been peaceful family neighborhoods. In the aftermath, affluent Black families soon followed their white neighbors and moved to unincorporated areas of Los Angeles County and cities such as Inglewood and Carson. Businesses were shuttered and factories closed, plunging Compton into the same poverty that its residents had once hoped to escape.

In just two decades Compton went from being predominantly white into the 1970s when it became majority Black. The decade would see the rise of street gangs like the Crips, an umbrella organization that in 1978 was made up of forty-five separate gangs (or "sets") operating in South Central Los Angeles on its way toward national expansion, becoming the fastest-growing gang in the '80s when movies like *Colors* glamorized gang life. In areas with rampant unemployment and poverty like Compton, these gangs were attractive because of the money that could be made from slinging drugs like PCP, marijuana, and amphetamines. It was all good in the hood.

This was the life that Eazy-E fell into as he sold drugs in a dangerous place ("the trap") that became gang central. In the '80s, freebase cocaine (or crack) began to flood the area. It went by several street names but was generally known as "ready-rock" because it was already freebased with baking soda and ready to smoke. Rock came cheap compared to cocaine without the danger of making a traditional freebase. Everybody from the era remembers comedian Richard Pryor running through the streets on fire. The open-air drug markets of Compton were the place to score as tons of cocaine were brought in by high-profile drug traffickers like "Freeway" Rick Ross and "Waterhead Bo" Bennet and distributed at the street level by gang members like Eazy-E.

The influence of the crack epidemic brought money to the poverty-stricken streets. It was a major come up for the denizens of the block. Being in a gang was no longer just about neighborhood pride, brotherhood, and protection—it became a means to get money and potentially escape the hood. Gang members and drug dealers displayed their new riches in the form of stylish clothes and flashy cars, which in turn influenced the next generation to admire these street legends (and follow them into a criminal lifestyle that seemed to offer an escape).

Life was cheap in the hood, but Eazy-E thrived as a dealer despite his short stature. Unlike many of his neighborhood peers, he didn't drink malt liquor or use drugs. Eazy remained sober to keep a sharp mental edge to his hustling. He needed to be taken seriously. While he enjoyed the benefits of the drug trade like the freshest threads and vehicles such as a Nissan truck, Suzuki Samurai, and a 1973 Chevy Caprice, he did his best to keep a low-profile as he bagged up his product in his parents' garage and drove to the Atlantic Drive apartment where he put in his work.

The primary tool of his trade was a beeper, which flashed numerical codes like "8" indicating that someone wanted an eight-ball of cocaine. He kept a couple grand stashed in his tube socks, and the rest of his earnings he kept in various spots, including his parents' garage. Always a ladies' man, he spent much of his income on extravagant gifts for a revolving cast of girlfriends. A true player that stunted on the streets of LA.

"[Eazy-E] was like a lotta other young people in the '80s, when cocaine was off the hook," explained Matt McDaniel, a local filmmaker who chronicled the emergence of the West Coast rap scene. "People were selling cocaine and making a lot of money. He was the first person that came out and admitted it and boasted about it on record."

In the early '80s, Eric had stacked his money and legend has it that by the age of twenty-two he had over a quarter million in cash from dealing drugs. That was a lot of money in 1986 and put Eazy-E on big-boy status as he lived the life of the neighborhood dope man, but a tragedy would have him reconsidering his profession.

His first cousin and mentor in the drug trade, Horace Butler, was shot and killed by seven bullets in a drive-by shooting. Eazy-E knew it was only a matter of time before prison or death caught up with him, following Butler's path. "I'd probably be dead right along with him," recalled Eazy-E in an interview with *Yo! MTV Raps*. "I figured I could do something else or I'd end up dead myself or in jail." Eazy didn't want to be judged by twelve or carried by six.

The Los Angeles hip-hop scene was growing rapidly in the mid-'80s and Eazy took an interest. He hosted parties with area DJs including Dr. Dre, sold mixtapes, and considered opening a record store, but all of that failed to offer the kind of money he could get dealing drugs. Eazy knew that to make millions, he'd have to produce his own rap records. He wanted to be the gangsta version of Motown's Barry Gordy. An OG of the rap game.

At the time, most records were coming out of the East Coast, and the rap songs that followed the disco era were mostly about partying, dancing, and having fun. Eazy had an idea to make songs about the reality that he was living. He wanted to tell it from the dope dealer's perspective. Again, his parents' garage would be the workshop for the young entrepreneur as he began using it as a makeshift studio to record mixtapes. While he wasn't the originator of the West Coast gangsta style that was being introduced by Toddy Tee with "Batterram" and Ice T with "6 in the Mornin'," Eazy would take "reality rap" to outrageous new levels and mainstream attention under the banner of his label, Ruthless Records, the most dangerous record label in the world.

Eazy-E had a vision to become "The Godfather of Gangsta Rap," as he was later acknowledged by TV talk-show host Arsenio Hall. He would become a songwriter, record producer, and entrepreneur who propelled the rise of West Coast gangsta rap by being the lead vocalist for N.W.A., founding Ruthless Records, and never shying away from his drug-dealing past, which he played up for the media and suburban white kids who loved the lurid tales of inner-city violence and criminality. To them Eazy-E was a straight thug personified.

While Eazy-E wasn't a great writer and lacked the lyrical finesse of established MCs, he had the business acumen to bring in others who could help him realize his vision. Most important, he had the image down with his signature drug-dealer style—dark glasses (called "Locs"), white T-shirt, khakis, and flashy cars. He would bring in writers to write the raps that complimented the thug template he portrayed and to give life to the street stories he lived. Eazy-E relished being the front man.

The original idea Eazy had was to start a label to promote his music. He was already making mixtapes. He was in the mix on the streets. He just moved from the street corner to the recording studio. He was using accumulated drug money to invest in recording equipment he had at his parents' home and to later buy studio time and get his records pressed. He was flipping his ill-gotten gains into a legitimate venture. A venture that would bring him fame, stature, and riches.

N.W.A. stood, of course, for "Niggaz Wit Attitudes," and the newly formed outfit carried the tagline "the world's most dangerous group." The lineup consisted of Eazy-E as their front-man rapper along with Ice Cube, Arabian Prince, DJ Yella, Dr. Dre, and MC Ren. They released their first single, "Boyz-n-the-Hood," on the Macola Records label. The single hit big on local KJAM radio before word went out to other places via Macola's distribution network, bootleg tapes, and radio recordings.

A compilation record with "Boyz-n-the-Hood," early N.W.A. demos, and some Dr. Dre cuts was released as N.W.A. *and the Posse* and went gold, mostly in mom-and-pop record shops, out-of-trunk sellers, and swap-meet vendors. There was something new coming up from the rap underground. It was truly a DIY movement. But Eazy knew he had to look outside Compton to establish N.W.A. nationwide. He had a vision of world domination.

To do so, he paid $750 for a meeting with a Beverly Hills music manager named Jerry Heller who was working with Dr. Dre and the World Class Wreckin' Cru. Eazy simply handed Heller a cassette and let his music speak for itself. After hearing an early cut of "Boyz-n-the-Hood" and a couple of other demos, the two went into business. Eazy took an 80 percent ownership stake, with Heller taking 20 percent. Eazy-E had to be in control of his Ruthless Records and make sure it lived up to the name. He was the street hustler; he was the gangsta; he was the product. And he had invested most of his drug money in this project.

Eazy worked on his debut album *Eazy-Duz-It*, which was written mostly by rappers MC Ren, Ice Cube, and The D.O.C., and produced by Dr. Dre and DJ Yella. It was released in September of 1988 featuring twelve tracks with cuts like "We Want Eazy," "Ruthless Villain," and "Boyz-n-the-Hood" amongst other gangsta songs that established his signature style.

The street hustler had made the transition to rap and became a player in the burgeoning industry. The album was labeled West Coast gangsta rap and sold over 2.5 million copies, hitting number 41 on the Billboard Top 200. That album paved the way for N.W.A.'s debut controversial album, *Straight Outta Compton.*

"Eazy's whole thing was: We've gotta put Compton on the map," Ice Cube told *Rolling Stone.* "Even people in LA was embarrassed to say they were from Compton. Compton was just like the worst of the worst. He was like, 'Man, motherfuckers yelling about their Brooklyn shit all the time, motherfuckers yelling the Bronx, motherfuckers yelling out their— we should yell out Compton,' so that was kind of how it happened."

Released in 1988, *Straight Outta Compton* was one of the most groundbreaking and infamous albums ever released. It featured songs depicting the world of drug dealing, partying, disrespecting women (calling them bitches), shootings, drive-bys, and killings. One of the songs that caused the most controversy was titled "Fuck tha Police," a sentiment that bubbled up during the Watts Rebellion, was shouted during the Rodney King Riots, and decades later exploded anew amid the Black Lives Matter movement.

It was a blatant middle finger to law enforcement and the racial injustice, systemic oppression, and the targeting of young Black males by the criminal justice system. The song caused disturbances across America and sometimes even riots. It became a slogan that was used by many African Americans and Latinos who were greatly influenced by and embedded in hip-hop culture. Even middle-class white kids felt liberated by the song, screaming "fuck the police" even if they didn't understand all its social ramifications.

In response, Milt Ahlerich, assistant director of the FBI's Department of Public Affairs, sent a strongly worded letter to Eazy-E's Ruthless Records voicing his concerns over the song. "Advocating violence and assault is wrong, and we in the law enforcement community take exception to such action," he wrote. "Music plays a significant role in our society and I wanted you to be aware of the FBI's position relative to this song and its message. I believe my views reflect the opinion of the entire law enforcement community."

It did seem that law enforcement had a target on Eazy-E and N.W.A. The G Street Express, which handled local promotion for the group, experienced continual problems booking shows for the tour. "We had thirty-six dates and all had problems in some way," G Street Express vice president Carol Kirkendall told the *Washington Post*. Some local police refused to work N.W.A.'s performances, requiring private security to be hired. Many venues made sure their contract prohibited the group from performing "Fuck tha Police."

After getting into a dispute with police in Detroit, who initially refused to work the show, Eazy-E and N.W.A. went ahead and performed the song, which caused police to rush the stage. Event security fought plainclothes cops. Scuffles backstage followed as the police attempted to arrest the group. In the aftermath, concert promoters in other cities were scared to book N.W.A. They were undeniably living up to the nickname of "the most dangerous group in the world" and kept it one hundred on the gangsta tip, bringing Los Angeles street and gang culture to the masses.

"They stereotype you and mess with you because you got a beeper, a little gold, and a nice car," Eazy-E told *Spin* magazine in 1990. "They figure you're a drug dealer or gang member. We're not telling anybody to join a gang or do drive-by shootings or to rob, steal, and kill. We're just telling how it is in Compton."

As the song brought the attention of law enforcement, it also brought increased media exposure to the group. Some saw the backlash against the song as a violation of the Constitution. Barry Lynn, legislative counsel for the American Civil Liberties Union, said that the FBI's threatening letter was "designed to get Priority [Records] to change its practices, policies, and distribution for the record and that's the kind of censorship by intimidation that the First Amendment doesn't permit." Similar support came from San Jose congressman Donald Edwards, who was a civil rights advocate. Either for or against N.W.A., all that mattered to Eazy-E was that they were making headlines and selling records.

"We're a group that demands and deserves respect," Eazy-E told *Shark* magazine. "There's still some people that don't give us the respect that we demand. There's no ifs, ands, or buts. You give us our respect. We sell a lot of records. We like real people; we don't deal with fake people. We're not fake people."

He continued: "When we go out, we go out and do what we want to do. You got something to say, word-up, just don't fuck with me. You don't like what I'm sayin', fuck you. You don't like how I'm living, well fuck you! As I've said."

Eazy-E was playing the role he was born to play. He had envisioned this success while he was still on the streets of Compton selling drugs, but now it had become a larger-than-life reality. The ensuing controversy only served to get N.W.A.'s and Eazy-E's name out and explosive record sales followed. Even with record stations and MTV refusing to play the singles, *Straight Outta Compton* quickly sold over one million copies, making it gangsta rap's first platinum certification. The album would hit number 9 on Billboard's Top R&B/Hip-Hop chart and number 37 on the Billboard 200 popular albums. By 1988 the album had sold over three million copies, making it triple platinum. It accomplished all of this with limited radio play and no initial support from MTV or BET.

Because of contractual and money disputes, Ice Cube, who wrote most of Eazy-E's lyrics, left the group in 1989 to start a successful solo career. This was a big blow to N.W.A., but they continued as a four-man group with Eazy-E, MC Ren, Dr. Dre, and DJ Yella. A rap feud started between N.W.A. and Ice Cube. In a 1990 *Spin* feature titled "N.W.A.: Hanging Tough," Ice Cube cites financial problems with Ruthless manager Jerry Heller. "Jerry's making all the money, and I'm not," claimed Cube. "Jerry has no creative input into the group: he just makes all the fucked-up decisions and gets all the fucking money." In the same article, Eazy-E refused to comment on Cube's accusations, choosing to save any response for N.W.A.'s upcoming *100 Miles and Runnin'* EP.

"It started with five but yo, one couldn't take it," Dre took a dig toward Cube in the opening title track "100 Miles." Later in the song "Real Niggaz," they liken Cube to notorious traitor Benedict Arnold. On his follow-up album *Death Certificate*, Cube responded with the song "No Vaseline," a five-minute diatribe against his old group. "You ran a hundred miles but you still got one to go," he snarled. "You're getting fucked by a white boy with no Vaseline." The verbal sparring spilled over into interviews and magazine articles, and through it all Eazy-E thrived on the publicity. Good or bad, it made no real difference as long as he was getting paid.

In 1991, N.W.A. released their final album as a group titled *Niggaz4Life*, which showed the musical brilliance of producer Dr. Dre. His style was a catchy blend of hooks from classic soul and funk records along with synthesizer riffs, which evolved the G-funk style first pioneered by the rap group Above the Law. The album went on to sell over two million copies in 1991 alone, making it double platinum. The group had reached its pinnacle.

In 1991, Eazy-E accepted an invitation to a lunch at the White House. It made the group larger than life. One day Eazy-E was screaming "Fuck tha Police," and the next day he got invited to the White House. All the news outlets covered it. Eazy was hailed as a marketing genius.

"We take all the different ideas and put them all into one. It gets mixed up different every time, according to each." Eazy-E told *Shark* magazine. "I was a businessman and a superhero. I want to go through it like this; I'm the executive producer."

N.W.A. started to split up as others in the group questioned Jerry Heller's management practices. They suspected something was wrong financially. Dr. Dre and The D.O.C. sent their new consultant, Marion "Suge" Knight, to look into Ruthless Records' finances as well as their contracts. Dr. Dre and The D.O.C. asked Eazy to release them from Ruthless Records. Eazy refused.

There were rumors about what actually happened between Suge Knight and Eazy-E. "Under threat of his life and telling him they would kill his mother—and that they were holding me as hostage—under those kinds of duress, [they] got him to sign releases for Dr. Dre," Heller recalled in his autobiography. Whatever the truth was, Eazy released Dr. Dre and The D.O.C from Ruthless. The two started their own label, Death Row Records, with Suge Knight, a football player turned bodyguard turned music mogul. It appeared that the street shit had come full circle. Threats and violence followed from Suge, but at Heller's prodding Eazy took the high road.

"Jerry told me that Eazy-E was intent on killing Suge Knight, something he discusses in his book, *Ruthless*," said S. Leigh Savidge, director of the documentary *Welcome to Death Row*. "Initially, when Jerry tried to talk him out of it, Eazy took it as a sign of Jerry's naivete—that he didn't understand what had to be done—that since Suge was trying to destroy everything that they had built—killing him was in line with the code of the street. Eventually Jerry talked him out of it."

As guards with machine guns were installed at the Ruthless Records office, Heller and Eazy-E would file a RICO lawsuit against Suge and Death Row that alleged money laundering, extortion, threats, and violent intimidation. It ended with a settlement that required Interscope Records—Death Row's financial backer and distributor—to pay to Ruthless a portion of the proceeds from Dr. Dre's future albums. For Eazy-E, it was better to have a piece of Dr. Dre than no Dre at all.

Dr. Dre's groundbreaking album *The Chronic* followed and featured a cut called "Dre Day." The video lampooned Eazy-E with an impersonator who stumbles around cartoonishly and gets chased by a gang. Eazy would get the last laugh, however, in his track "Real Muthaphuckkin G's," which mocked Dr. Dre's classic Wreckin' Cru sequined doctor's costume, lipstick, and eyeliner and labeled him a "studio gangsta." But, more important, Eazy made it known that the diss track " 'Dre Day' only made Eazy's payday."

"Eazy was getting like twenty-five or fifty cents a copy for Dre's *Chronic* album," explained Doug Young, a promoter for both Ruthless and Death Row. "That's why on Eazy's album, *187 Killer*, on that song " 'Dre Day' [only] made Eazy's payday", that's what he's talking about. . . . Every time 'Dre Day' sells a record, I get twenty-five cents a copy."

Resuming his solo career, Eazy-E released two EPs but stayed more relevant behind the scenes, as he signed to his label the Ohio rap group Bone Thugs-n-Harmony. Eazy-E took his role as kingmaker seriously as he became acknowledged as the godfather of gangsta rap. He was a drug dealer turned rap superstar who lived by and stuck to the codes of the street. Through it all he never turned his back on his past—instead he championed it. There was even talk of an N.W.A. reunion when tragedy struck.

On March 16, 1995, the world found out that Eazy had AIDS. As the rapper was on life support in an intensive care unit, his lawyer read a statement from Eazy to a press conference: "I may not seem like a guy you would pick to preach a sermon," Eazy began. "Yeah, I was the brother on the streets of Compton doing a lot of things most people look down on—but it did pay off. Then we started rapping about real stuff that shook up the LAPD and FBI, but we got our message across big time and everyone in America started paying attention to the boys in the 'hood.' "

Eazy-E was buried on April 7, 1995, at Rose Hills Memorial Park in Whittier, California. Over three thousand people attended his funeral, including Jerry Heller and DJ Yella. He was laid to rest in a gold casket rocking his Compton signature baseball cap. He took real stories from the street and created a rap genre that would last forever. Eazy E set the template and remained a true G to the end.

THE DRUG KINGPIN BEHIN DEATH ROW

LA

Death Row Records and Harry-O

4

DEATH ROW RECORDS REMAINS INFAMOUS in hip-hop history. Established in 1992, the powerhouse label launched the solo career of Dr. Dre, brought Snoop Dogg to the world, and solidified a legacy with Tupac—all at the hands of notorious label head Suge Knight, a gangster who conducted business by any means necessary. From 1992 to 1998, Death Row ran the hip-hop charts and raked in millions of dollars, while at the same time stacking up prison sentences and even body counts as it launched an all-out war between the East and West Coast rap scenes. Today, many who were there refuse to talk about Suge. Even with him locked away behind bars until 2037, his shadow looms as large as his frame.

While the role Dr. Dre and Suge Knight played in the label's formation was well publicized, its criminal financial backing was shrouded in mystery. "It's always been a subject of speculation where they got their original funding," said Jeffery Jolson Colburn, music editor of the *Hollywood Reporter*. Jay King, host of *The Music Business: The Way I See It*, agrees, "There are so many things you heard about this situation. I'll tell you this, Mike Harris was firmly planted in the middle of it."

Michael "Harry-O" Harris was born on September 20, 1960, in Los Angeles in the section of South Central known as the "Low Bottoms." He was raised by his mother, who was a single parent working two jobs to take care of Michael and his brother. South Central was rough and the sharks roamed at will. "This place exists in every city," recalled Harry-O in an interview for the documentary *Welcome to Death Row*. "It was a while before I even realized that I was living in what they call the ghetto because I had nothing to compare it to."

All of Los Angeles was gang-infested by the '90s. There were hundreds of Blood and Crips sets, made up of kids born in LA in the late '60s and early '70s, that dominated the streets of their neighborhoods and ruled with impunity. The mix of low-income, poor, and middle-class families who were forced to live together in the same zip codes created a perfect situation that helped the gangs thrive. In a cauldron of violence and bravado, kids and teenagers learned the laws of the ghetto at the point of a gun.

Local news reporter Christian Blatford summarized Michael Harris as "a man drug agents describe as a major cocaine trafficker. At the young age of twenty-six, he had already made millions of dollars. [He comes from] the streets of South Central Los Angeles, where he started pushing dope on street corners and ran with a Blood street gang called the 'Bounty Hunters.' In the drug world, he is known as Harry-O."

Michael Harris, or "Harry-O," grew up to be respected and feared by both his peers and enemies. He had a sharp business mind when he entered the drug-dealing world. "I was not a drug dealer. I was a person who decided to deal drugs," explained Harry-O. "I just think we all had the same attitude—somebody's gotta do it. So we might as well do it. When somebody doesn't have anything, they'll do anything to get it." That's just the law of the jungle.

And "get it" he did as he started stacking his silver like a baron. "It was like a typhoon, and we all got swept up in it," Harry-O told the *New York Post*. "Some of us became addicted to drugs, and some of us became addicted to selling drugs, but we all became addicted, we all had some form of sickness." They called it "the game" but it was really a vicious trap that led to death and incarceration.

Despite his success, Harry-O was looking for an out, one that would help him go legitimate and maintain the level of recognition that he achieved in the streets. Harry-O's entrepreneurial skill extended beyond just selling drugs. He started investing his drug money in real estate and businesses that turned out to be very lucrative. He made a lot of cash, bought houses, cars, and anything else he wanted. But Harry-O remained firmly rooted in the drug game. He was addicted to the lifestyle, even though he'd flirted with the entertainment industry, straddling both worlds like a king.

"He had a limousine service. The people he picked up were in the entertainment field, a lot of celebrities—because everybody wanted limos," his wife Lydia Harris said in an interview for *Welcome to Death Row*. "I worked closely with people like Denzel Washington in the beginning when he was getting his career off the ground," added Harry-O. "I just worked with him. I was in a position to help him." The hood supports its own.

But his attempt to jump from the street to become Mr. Hollywood would be short-lived. By 1989, Harry-O was convicted in California Superior Court of attempted murder, kidnapping, and conspiracy to commit murder. He was sentenced to twenty-five years to life. The following year a federal jury convicted him of cocaine trafficking, and he was sentenced to another twenty-five years. It looked like he was finished. But all his life, both in and out of prison, Harry-O had always made moves and he was about to make his biggest when Suge Knight entered the picture.

Marion Hugh Knight Jr. was born April 19, 1965, in Compton, California, a rough city in South Los Angeles County, south of downtown LA, made famous by gangsta rappers N.W.A. and DJ Quik. Marion was called "Sugar Bear" as a kid because of his big size. Later it was shortened to "Suge." Growing up in Compton, Suge hung around a Piru Bloods set and considered them friends but didn't join because of his football ambitions. His homies saw his potential to make it out of the trap.

Suge played football throughout high school and when he graduated and went to college he first attended and played for two-year El Camino in Torrance, California, before he transferred to the University of Nevada, Las Vegas, to play defensive end and get on the radar of NFL scouts. Suge boasted, "I used to go to football practice in college and see how many teammates I could hurt." But the young man was as dangerous on the street as he was on the football field.

In 1987, an offer to play for the San Francisco 49ers was rescinded when Suge was arrested in an altercation with a friend. He was charged with attempted murder and grand theft auto for shooting his friend and stealing his car. He was able to plead down to misdemeanors and three years' probation, but the 49ers had grown cold toward signing him. Suge's dream was crushed, but he got another shot with the LA Rams and played a couple games for them, albeit while their regular team was on strike.

Because of Suge's immense size, six feet two and 265 pounds of solid muscle that he carried well, he started a side hustle as a bodyguard for celebrities such as R&B singer Bobby Brown. At this time he became acquainted with N.W.A. through lyric writer D.O.C. "Suge got off on that shit; it was fun to him," explained D.O.C. "If I got drunk and slapped a girl's ass, and her guy got upset, Suge would beat the motherfucker up and then we'd just leave."

Being around people like Brown and becoming acquainted with the up-and-coming rappers, Suge began studying and learning the music industry and found that a lot of Black artists were getting robbed blind by white music executives. "I was up there looking and learning, you know," said Suge. "And I seen the different people complain. I seen artists. I seen people talking about songs. And I'm just listening and hearing it all. I investigated and found out who do the writin' and the music and how do they get paid? So that's when I started my publishing company and signin' writers."

One of the first to sign was Mario Johnson, aka "Chocolate," who claimed to have written songs for Vanilla Ice, including his breakout rap single "Ice, Ice Baby." When Suge learned that Mario wasn't getting paid, he set out to get the publishing rights through some unorthodox means. Street legend has it that Suge manhandled Vanilla Ice and hung him by his ankles off a hotel balcony eighteen floors high to force him to sign over points on the song. The truth is only mildly tamer.

Suge recalled the encounter, "I'm like, 'You can't give me nothing. It's what I'm going to do to you because you didn't get the rights to put it out there; because I haven't gotten paid and my client hasn't gotten paid.'" Vanilla Ice said, "Suge took me out on the balcony, started to talk to me personally. He had me look over the edge, showing me how high I was up there. . . . I needed to wear a diaper that day." However it went down, the tactic was effective, and Suge and Chocolate got rights to songs worth millions.

It was through The D.O.C. that Suge met N.W.A. and befriended Andre "Dr. Dre" Young, one of the main creative forces behind N.W.A.'s music and sound. It was all coming together for Suge. He was gaining valuable experience, forging friendships, and formulating a plan to take over the rap game—but he needed money if he wanted to put his grand plan into effect.

At the time, N.W.A. was having problems with their label Ruthless Records, which was owned and operated by Eazy-E and his business partner Jerry Heller. "They had Dre doin' all this work and makin' all these great songs and they wasn't payin' him what he was worth," said Suge. "Matter of fact, they weren't payin' him at all."

Suge brought D.O.C. and Dre to Dick Griffey, the owner of Solar Records, to review their contract with Ruthless. "I'm telling D.O.C. and Dre—I don't know who you guys are—I don't know your music. I don't particularly care for it," said Griffey. "But if somebody's selling it, you deserve to be paid. You deserve to maximize your opportunities. So let me show you how to do this."

Dr. Dre, Dick Griffey, The D.O.C., and Suge Knight wanted to start their own hip-hop label. They knew they had something special, and that Dr. Dre was the man behind Ruthless Records' success and hits. With The D.O.C. on board to write the rhymes, their label couldn't miss. But the problem remained that Dre was still under contract with Ruthless, and getting him out would once again require Suge's strong-arm methods.

Suge—with his knowledge of contracts plus street tactics of using threats, intimidation, and violence—got Dr. Dre released from his obligations to Ruthless Records. Like the incident with Vanilla Ice, the infamous altercation between Suge, Eazy-E, and Jerry Heller has also become embellished street lore. Some say that Eazy-E was bludgeoned. Eazy-E's widow Tomica Woods-Wright claims he was lured to the Solar Studios by Dr. Dre. There he was met in the elevator by Suge Knight, who led him into a room with several men carrying baseball bats.

Everything was set with Dre clear, but Suge still didn't have the money to start the project and secure a studio in the Solar building for Death Row to record. Meanwhile, Harry-O still had lots of time to do, but he was looking to make some investments. His wife Lydia was a singer, and Harry-O was interested in making an album. His cellmate at the time, "Freeway" Ricky Ross, had read in magazines that Dr. Dre had fallen out with Ruthless Records and suggested, "Why don't you let Dre produce Lydia? Now you'll have a hit on your hands and Dre need the money."

But from behind bars with limited phone time, neither man was able to get in touch with Dre. Suge was easier to get in touch with. Harry-O reached Suge through a mutual acquaintance and Suge was put in contact with Harris's attorney, David Kenner. Through Kenner, Suge visited Harry-O, who had been locked up for a couple of years but still had cash from his kingpin days and was eager to get involved in the music scene.

Harry-O recalled their first meeting in prison: "When I asked the question, 'What does it actually take?' Suge told me we could be fifty-fifty partners for about a million-five." It seemed to be a good match because Suge and Harry-O both wanted to break into entertainment and knew they had a golden goose with Dr. Dre. "We started talking with Suge, and Mike [Harry-O] said, 'You got Dre?' and Suge said, 'Yeah, the hit producer.'"

Terms were discussed and agreed to. Harry-O ended up financing Death Row Records with a $1.5 million investment made through his company Godfather Entertainment, which he'd set up with his attorney and business partner David Kenner. "David was the legal mind. Suge was handling the day-to-day stuff. And I would provide the overall business strategy and connection to the streets," said Harry-O.

"A couple of days after Mrs. Harris and David Kenner came in, things started to change drastically. Immediately the studio gets carpeted, things start getting fixed," recalled John Payne, sound engineer at Death Row. But it wasn't just the wall-to-wall bloodred carpet that was new to the Solar studio, Harry-O had installed a phone line exclusively for him to call in from prison on a hidden cell phone or through the prison system. "There was a phone in the studio reserved for me to call on. Suge made it clear that the phone should not be tied up," Harry-O said. Label artists and Def Row employees such as Jewell and Snoop Dog became accustomed to picking up the ringing phone and hearing, "You are receiving a call from an inmate at California State Prison." They knew to say yes, though they may or may not have been aware that the voice behind bars was paying for their apartments and helping them out with their own legal battles.

Death Row Records of course went on to produce some of the biggest records in hip-hop's history, starting with *The Chronic* by Dr. Dre, Snoop Dogg's *Doggystyle*, and Tupac's *All Eyez On Me*. And with a lineup of other artists such as Nate Dogg, Daz Dillinger, Kurupt, and The D.O.C., the label sold over 150 million albums and made over $750 million.

During the early days, Death Row was the biggest rap label in the world. Suge Knight paid the legal fees to get Snoop Dogg acquitted of murder and he also helped secure Tupac's release from prison following a sexual-assault conviction. But the label waned after Tupac got shot dead in Las Vegas and Snoop Dogg, Dr. Dre, and others left Death Row.

After the label rose to fame (or infamy), Harry-O found himself being more and more sidelined by Suge. He was kept out of the courting of

Interscope Records, only learning about it through industry magazines sent to his prison cell. As a sign of the falling out, Harry-O's direct phone line to the Death Row offices was removed. Harry-O claimed there was an element of jealousy. "People would say, 'That's Harry-O's company,'" he said. "[Suge] could not stand tall if I was in the picture. At first it was okay because (Death Row) needed to be connected to the street element. Then things changed. . . . Once Suge got a taste of the spotlight, he wanted it all by himself. If Suge didn't want to be my partner, I didn't have a problem with that. But at least compensate me for my time and monies invested." Harry-O ended up taking Suge Knight to court because of a financial dispute and won.

Harry-O remained active behind bars but turned his attention to more philanthropic endeavors. He brought the award-winning *San Quentin News* back from the brink of death and became its editor. He was also cofounder of "The Richmond Project," a nonprofit that aimed to prevent youth in West Contra Costa from getting into the crime game that had robbed Harry-O of his freedom.

"I've been in prison with crack babies, their parents are people who consumed the drugs that me and so many other people sold. And I had to sit with them, I had to talk to them, I had to see the results of what we did," Harry-O told the *New York Post*. "Every day, even now, I think about my participation and it makes me sick to my stomach. That's killing me even today."

Suge Knight fell from grace and ended up in jail. In September 2018, after pleading no contest to voluntary manslaughter in a fatal 2015 hit-and-run incident that occurred after Suge made an unauthorized visit to the set of the N.W.A. docudrama *Straight Outta Compton*. Suge was sentenced to twenty-eight years. He is scheduled to become eligible for parole in July 2037. Death Row Records filed for bankruptcy and went through various owners, including the toy company Hasbro. It was most recently purchased by Death Row alumnus Snoop Dogg.

Michael "Harry-O" Harris's sentence was commuted by President Donald Trump on January 19, 2021, during his final days in office. Harris served thirty years. He's now out, free in the world and plotting his next move. A notorious figure who was buried inside the belly of the beast has now emerged to take his rightful place in the top echelon of hip-hop infamy.

THE GANGSTAS FROM LITTLE HAITI

MIA

Zoe Nation and Zoe Pound

5

MIAMI, FLORIDA. ONE OF THE UNITED STATES' most luxurious hot spots. A city that attracts celebrities and high rollers and hood stars from all over. People from all cultures, nationalities, and backgrounds mingle and party with the rich and famous—but that's all on one side of the bridge.

Once you cross over, you enter a new world. There, the poor fight for survival in a cold, hard, rough city. Welcome to Miami Beach. The hood—where Blacks, Jamaicans, Cubans, Puerto Ricans, and others bubbled up in the same boiling cauldron. And then there is Little Haiti. It's a dangerous spot and home to one of Florida's most violent street gangs—the Zoe Pound. From humble beginnings they came up through robberies, drug deals, and hustles to make power moves in the world of hip-hop.

From the '70s to the '90's Haitians fled the island to escape the brutal rule of Francois "Papa Doc" Duvalier and his successor, Jean Claude Duvalier or "Baby Doc." Papa Doc was notorious for using death squads to kill political opponents. He would run unopposed in sham elections and eventually declared himself "President for Life." After his death, his son, Baby Doc, instituted some cosmetic changes to the regime but continued to use deadly force and torture to maintain his iron grip on the country. The people feared speaking out against the president, even in private. Often they'd rather risk the seven-hundred-mile ocean journey on ramshackle boats and makeshift rafts in a life-or-death attempt to make it to the sands of Miami beach.

"Life in Haiti is the real hard-knock life. The poverty level is real bad. There are no jobs and people are struggling," Mac-A-Zoe, who's serving life for murder and robberies, told *Don Diva Magazine*. "There is no food and there is no way of providing for their family. It's rough. They want to do the right thing but there is nothing coming from doing the right thing. There is a lot of madness and killing going on right now in Haiti because of all this. They committing robberies and kidnappings, people are hungry and they are going to eat."

The refugees settled in "Little Haiti," a poor neighborhood in Miami, north of downtown. It has four zip codes and covers just under three and a half square miles. Victor Juste, a prominent Haitian businessman and community leader, came up with the name Little Haiti. Finding food, clothes, and shelter as well as a steady job wasn't that easy for the Haitian immigrants. Most had to start from nothing and it was a difficult struggle, even though it was much easier than what they escaped from at home. Despite the hardships, they knew they had come far and things could only get better for them and their children.

"By the early 1990s, Miami had the fourth-highest percentage of residents in poverty out of all major U.S. cities. In parts of Liberty City, 68 percent of the families were living in poverty," explained famous Miami rapper Luther "Uncle Luke" Campbell in his autobiography *The Book of Luke: My Fight for Truth, Justice, and Liberty City*. "To make matters worse, Miami also started seeing a massive surge in immigration from Haiti. Thousands of Haitians descended on Florida trying to escape the torture and killings of the Duvalier regime back home. New Haitian gangs like Zombie Boys, E-Unit, Zoe Pound, and several others exacerbated the problems."

While the parents struggled to find work, their children battled to be accepted at the schools. The outsiders were teased and picked on for being poor and wearing second-hand clothes. "It is still hard, but it was harder before," Mac-A-Zoe said. "During the '70s and '80s, Haitian immigrants were misunderstood. We were looked at as outcasts even by other Black people. Though we were Black too, we were different. We even spoke a different language, had different beliefs and religion. That brought a little pressure. Even going to school we had it rough. They had this thing called 'Haitian Fridays' . . . every Friday they would beat on the Haitians."

The Haitian kids wanted better and didn't know how to do better— they were still children. They were being preyed on by others. They knew if they wanted to survive and make it, they had to fight back. As a culture, they believed that strength was in unity. It ran in their blood—down to their bone. So they cliqued up and retaliated. The Haitian kids were different when it came to violence. They had a carefree attitude toward it. The young Haitians began as victims, being teased, chased, and picked on, but slowly they turned the tide until they were the aggressors doing what was done to them to the same ones who picked on them before. They were proving the point that they weren't the ones to be fucked with. They also took advantage of that by robbing and extorting other kids to get money.

From this culture came one gang that would rise above them all and make waves beyond the few miles of Little Haiti. In an appearance on *David Letterman*, Wyclef Jean of the hip-hop group the Fugees would hold up a Haitian flag and call out "Zoe for life." Letterman's national audience may not have been aware that he was name-dropping Miami's most violent criminal gang, but to those in the know, it was a call to Haitian nationalism, a movement that Zoe Pound had fostered in the streets. Each member was said to be dangerous, heartless, and ready to commit murder—but above all they promoted Haitian unity and pride.

There are various stories about how Zoe Pound was created and what the name represented. According to founding member Ali "Zoe" Adam, it was organized by a gangster named Chubb who was tight with some of the original Haitian street cliques like the Sable Palm Boys and the Carol City Haitians. "It was Chubb," recalled Ali. "He started the White House with only four ounces, and together, we turned it into a symbol of power and Haitian pride. Chubb was the original leader of Zoe Pound. He had everyone's respect and was worthy of the title."

The word "Zoe" is a variant of "zo," which in Haitian-Creole means "bone." Embracing that word came to be a way of saying they were tough down to their very core—the bone. Some suggest that Pound represented the kilos of cocaine they were bringing in and distributing. Others say that it came about when they were listening to Snoop Dogg's spin-off group Tha Dogg Pound and Chubb stood up and yelled, "Fuck the Dogg Pound! It's all about the Zoe Pound." Being part of the Zoe Pound was often simply a matter of being Haitian and ready to take it to the next level and represent the island nation in the street. The organization was a loose affiliation of those who had the same goals and desires. A leader in the group was someone who simply made a name from their criminal work and gained respect from others. They didn't get tattoos or flash gang signs, and the only colors they rocked were that of Haiti—red and blue.

"Zoe Pound is far from a gang," Mac-A-Zoe told *Don Diva*. "We are a movement. We fight for the cause; we fight for what is right. We are heavily connected to the streets. I come from the streets so it's going to be hard for me to not embrace brothers in the streets. I gotta always embrace the struggle. That is what made me. That is what made the Zoe Pound."

By the mid-'90s, the Zoe Pound was one of the largest gangs in Florida, with more than a thousand different sets. The gangs started out stealing cargo from the Port of Miami, then they switched to robbing the cargo freighters by force with weapons. A lot of these freighters were smuggling drugs into the United States through the port. The gangs learned of this through tips back home and robbed these ships as they came in. Often the drugs would be well hidden in the hull of the ship to escape customs. Finding out their location would require torturing the crew until they spilled their guts—sometimes literally. A single heist could net millions of dollars of cocaine that was then sold in the street. The Zoes also engaged in home invasions, murders, and robberies. Zoe Pound was all over the news just as they were trying to make a move into the rap game.

Zoe Pound was about branding from the jump. From their headquarters at the corner of 56th Street and Northeast 1st Avenue dubbed the "White House," they would put the name "Zoe Pound" on all of their drug merchandise. It was Chubb's idea to publicize the gang further by forming a rap group called Zoe Pound that featured members Mac-A-Zoe, Red Eyez, G-Glind, and Blind. Through this street marketing, the notoriety and name of Zoe Pound spread so that even in places like New York and California, Haitians were puffing out their chests with pride and claiming to be Zoe. It was not just a gang but a political-identity movement.

As the Zoes gained money, power, and respect, they started making a name in hip-hop as well. Trick Daddy, a Miami-Dade County rapper, acknowledged their notoriety in his track "Round Here," calling out, "It's the season of the Zoes round here." Ali and Zoe Pound helped book a Miami show for a young group of Haitians who became known as the Fugees. Wyclef Jean of the Fugees remained close and released videos for "Thug Angels" and "M.V.P." that featured Mac-A-Zoe and other members in Zoe Pound T-shirts.

They set the style wearing the Haiti national flag as bandanas as they drove around in "dunks"—old-school Chevys covered with bright candy paint and outfitted with oversized rims and booming sound systems. They'd drive around waving their flags and shouting out Zoe Pound. Their wealth and notoriety brought VIP access to Miami's nicest restaurants, dance clubs, and strip clubs like Rolex, where the old-money Miami elite were dismayed by the spectacle of the Zoe boys showering their snow bunnies with dollar bills.

"The nigga that started 'make it rain' was Zoe," claims rapper and Zoe Pound affiliate Jim Jones in a radio interview. "Miami. Zoe Pound Boys. Going down there. Rolex. Five thousand. Flicking that shit. *Whaaa, whaaa, whaaaa*! That shit started down there in Miami."

It spread, and before long numerous rap videos showed showers of dollar bills raining down on strippers and from there the activity went to all the regional strip clubs. Everyone was makin' it rain! After the shooting death of de facto leader Chubb, Ali "Chip" Adam took over as the face of the gang. Ali was born in Jereme, Haiti, and came to the United States at the age of nine, growing up in Little Haiti. As he got older and robbing the boats at the ports got too dangerous, Ali Adam, who became known as "Ali Zoe," began to import cocaine from Haiti. According to court records, Ali had loads of cocaine shipped by boat coming in through the Port of Miami and in suitcases flown into South Florida on American Airlines flights. His pickup man testified that these suitcases contained between 140 and 180 kilos of cocaine.

"Chip [Ali Zoe] prevailing unscathed after numerous shoot-outs and his nineteen-year criminal run most certainly qualifies him to provide the urban community with some insight on the dos and don'ts of the 'game,' " explained journalist Jermaine Atkins in his book *Zoe Pound Mafia*. "Some attribute Chip's nine to a hundred lives and success to the practices of voodoo. [And] when you do the math, via amassing a multimillion-dollar fortune in a violent city like Miami and engaging in egregious criminal conduct for over nineteen years—without serving more than sixty-two days in jail or ever being shot—one might think Chip had a supernatural force watching out for him."

To say that Ali Zoe was not shy about flaunting his criminal success would be an understatement. He reveled in his role as "King of Miami" as he drove around in Lamborghinis and a Rolls-Royce Phantom as he worked to further get the Zoe Pound name out in the public sphere. He was able to convince the History Channel's docuseries *Gangland* to feature Zoe Pound and arranged interviews with Mac-A-Zoe, who was now behind bars for robbery and murder. His biggest avenue for publicity was in the hip-hop arena, however, as Ali Zoe emulated other street hustlers who went legit by becoming power brokers who sponsored the next hip-hop stars.

By 2004, Zoe Pound was the talk of the hip-hop industry and stars like Ludacris claimed that the only way to do Miami was as part of the Zoe entourage. When Louisiana's Cash Money Records came to town to record at Circle House Studios in Miami, they made sure to connect with the Zoe Pound. To be seen around town with the Zoe not only gave access to the finest the city had to offer, it granted protection. To mess with Cash Money was to mess with Zoe Pound, and nobody in their right mind was trying to do that. It is speculated that the Zoe Pound connection was how Cash Money were able to make five music videos in the projects around thugs and not get robbed for their millions of dollars of jewelry. Cash Money superstar Lil Wayne would rhyme on "Don't Trip," *I'm up in Lil Haiti / I'm blowing up Jamaica / I'm in the Pimp Beemer / I'm with a saltshaker / Where Zoe Pound at.*

In 2006, Ali started promoting a hip-hop artist named Bazil Knight, a street gangster who had spent seven and a half years in a Florida State Prison and had become known for his lyrical genius. He was no studio gangster; he rapped about the hard street life he knew all too well, and Ali Zoe was quick to sign him to his Lifeline Records. Ali Zoe wanted to cash in his accumulated favors and make sure that Bazil's album had enough big names involved to get attention from industry bigwigs. Rick Ross— coming fresh off his hit single "Hustlin'"—agreed to do a song with Bazil. Wyclef from the Fugees again proved his Zoe loyalties by adding some bars on a Bazil track. Hit producer Pharell contributed a beat as did rapper Scarface. The album would also include female hip-hop artist Jacki-O and reggae musician Ziggy Marley. All that was missing was for Cash Money's superstar Lil Wayne to pay back and appear on a single.

Legend has it that Lil Wayne rebuffed Ali Zoe's cordial advances until finally a fed-up Ali grabbed Lil Wayne by his necklaces and pushed him against a recording studio wall yelling, "a nigga done red-carpeted you sassy ass niggas around Miami and you think you can stay in Miami fuck nigga and not politick with a nigga!?" Zoe snatched Wayne's chain and left, but the drama soon spilled onto the streets. Within two days, sixty-seven shots were fired at the Cash Money tour bus and forty thousand flyers went out around town displaying AK-47s and the demand "Cash Money must leave Miami or show Miami love." Lil Wayne was hunted down at the Portofino Yacht Club and his 2007 Rolls-Royce Phantom was firebombed, an act of arson that is said to have been overseen by Ali Zoe himself.

Hip-hop had seen turf battles like this before, but as they did in Little Haiti, Zoe Pound took it to a whole new level. Part of this was the influence Ali Zoe was getting from some New York heavies who Wyclef Jean had introduced him to. Jimmy Henchman and Haitian Jack were known around the music industry as guys who used the old New York *mafioso* methods to strong-arm deals and get business done. They taught Ali that if he wanted to achieve greatness, he had to stop asking permission from the industry and start making things happen. But Jimmy Henchman was perhaps unprepared for the devil he had unleashed in Ali Zoe. In the middle of the Cash Money war, Jimmy flew to Miami to dead the issue. Henchman tried to calm Ali and explained that the violence would scare industry executives away and that it wasn't good for business. He retrieved Lil Wayne's chain and negotiated an appearance by Lil Wayne and Zoe Ali on DJ Khaled's radio show that night to make sure everybody knew that peace had been made.

But the strong-arm methods continued when Houston rapper Lil Flip bailed on a concert performance that had been partially set up and promoted by Zoe Pound. Ali Zoe demanded that Lil Flip perform a free show and pay $40,000 to the promoter to secure a safe relationship with South Florida. When Lil Flip balked, his 2004 Maserati Quattroporte was ambushed, and photographs were taken of the artist crying as pit bulls lunged at him and threats were made on his life. Zoe himself was at the scene and demanded a payment of $100,000; otherwise he would leak the pictures to the media. Later that night payment plus extra would be made and the incriminating disposable camera given to Lil Flip. It was clear that if you wanted to rap in South Florida, you did so only with Zoe Pound's permission.

Another famous altercation happened in New York involving rap mogul Sean "Puffy" Combs. Ali Zoe was promoting Harlem rapper Jim Jones, who had shown love for the Zoe in his single "Summer Wit

Miami," in which he rhymed *I'm with Zoe and G as I slide to the Rolex*. Jones was set to establish himself as the new rap king of Harlem at the same time Puffy was pumping money into reestablishing the career of the former crown holder, Mase. Puff called Ali directly to settle things and flew to Florida to meet up at Puff's four-story Star Island mansion. Puffy suggested he and Jim Jones make a track right there and shoot a video. The two disappeared into the recording studio to lay down "What You Been Drankin' On." The video, an ode to codeine-laced "lean" drank, featured Ali Zoe in the intro rolling up to a Little Haiti pub in his Porsche and ordering a "sizzurp." In addition to Jim Jones, Puff features on the track brandishing the Haitian flag bandana, proving his love for Miami and respect for Zoe Pound.

Whatever supernatural force was looking out for Ali Zoe vanished in 2007 when the feds' "Operation Zoe Pound" caught up with him. He was indicted by the feds on a continuing criminal enterprise charge in California, Florida, and New York City, where it was alleged he moved over 6,300 kilos of cocaine and laundered over $75 million (in addition to twelve other charges). He got life in federal prison, but it didn't stop him. He kept it moving even behind prison walls and negotiated a six-figure deal with Paramount Pictures to use the name "Zoe Pound" in their movie *Bad Boys*. An episode of the television show *American Greed* covered his life and ties with the South Florida "Bernie Madoff" Garry Souffront. Ali Zoe wrote several books, including a manifesto entitled *Hip-Hop Black Republican Party*. In it he takes the unity movement of Zoe Pound to new levels for his peoples by bringing them back to their original conservative roots. He continues to call for all performers, celebrities, and athletes of Haitian origins to come together to bring positive change to their birth nation.

But the Zoe Pound legacy is still felt in the clubs where they make it rain, and in hip-hop lore with the praise and love that comes from Lil Wayne, 50 Cent, Rick Ross, Lil Boosie, French Montana, Lil Durk, Future, Pitbull, and many others. Lil Wayne may have rapped it best in "Miss Me," rhyming *Shut the fuck up / real niggas talking / got to do it one time for Haiti / what up Zoe!*

PART 2

1990s

*The Glory
Years*

THE
BROOKLYN
DON
BK

Jay-Z and
Calvin Klein

6

NEW YORK CITY HAS OVER THREE HUNDRED housing projects scattered across its landscape. A blight on the bright, city lights where those living in a world of poverty and government assistance dwell. Denizens of the ghetto. The bottom rung of America's capitalist hierarchy.

Once called slums—and later called "the hood"—these areas were harsh, desolate, and often brutal, and through the '50s and '60s they were flooded with gladiatorial gang culture. Violence increased in the five boroughs, but after a time groups emerged to stem the gangs. At the time these gangs were more likely to fight with fists and occasionally knives than handguns and assault rifles. Sometimes a *West Side Story*–style dance-off might be enough to settle a block dispute. They had colorful names like the Black Spades, Savage Skulls, Chingalings, Black Falcons, and Golden Guineas brandished on the backs of their jean jackets with cutoff sleeves. They advertised by tagging walls and subways with their gang affiliation and street names.

In the 1970s gang violence exploded and handguns, grenades, and even machine guns were introduced. In 1971, a bloody escalation between the larger gangs—such as the Ghetto Brothers, Black Spades, and Savage Skulls—had gang members and social workers alike seeking to make peace. In a highly publicized event, the leaders of the gangs sat down with a Boys Club director and priest to map out a peace treaty. The media took pictures as the gangs huddled and yelled "Peace!" Meanwhile, the NYPD's Bronx Youth Gang Task Force had little hope for peace and was setting up shop and ready to clean up the streets of any gang activity. "With some thirty thousand cops, we got the biggest gang in the city. You're going to lose," said one officer in an interview with the *New York Post*.

This Bronx setting was ground zero for the explosion of what would become known as hip-hop, which incorporated four different street arts—emceeing, deejaying, graffiti tagging, and break dancing. In the late '80s and early '90s, hip-hop would become violent, as gangsta rap emerged with lurid tales of shoot-outs between rival "colors." But in the early days, hip-hop was all about unity and peace across gangs. And although petty theft and fisticuffs may have been a way of life in the hood, at the end of the day everybody just wanted to get down.

And in the Bronx, the place to get down was at a party presided over by Clive Campbell, aka DJ Kool Herc. The most legendary one took place in an apartment building rec room where a young Clive made his name. His sister was only making forty-five dollars a week at her job and needed a lot more to buy back-to-school clothes from the trendy shops on Delancey Street. She did the math and decided her hustle would be to take what money she had to buy malt liquor and soda and get her brother Clive to play a DJ set. By charging a modest cover charge and selling refreshments, she could fill the room and go back to school with a new wardrobe. Her hustle launched a career.

"Hip-hop started when my father brought a PA system and didn't know how to hook it up," DJ Kool Herc told Davey D at the New Music Seminar in 1989. "I was messing around with the music, and I started out by buying a few records to play at my house. When I was doing that, I saw a lot of kids playing outside in the backyard. My sister asked me to give a party one day. I went out and got around twenty records that I felt was good enough and we gave a party."

Deejaying was in Clive Campbell's blood, as his Jamaican parents were familiar with the dancehall scene. He vividly remembered the men unloading the massive sound systems that would lure in all the gangsters and famous people. In the Bronx, Clive got his start by rigging up the family's home stereo system to his father's PA system, which increased its power dramatically. His father couldn't be mad. "Rass claat, man! We 'ave sound!!!" he declared. The boy would accompany his father and deejay between R&B sets in exchange for being able to use the equipment for his own parties. He'd take his DJ name from his graffiti tag, "CLYDE AS KOOL," and his school nickname, "Hercules," given because of his muscular frame. DJ Kool Herc was born, and he was ready to launch what would become hip-hop.

The breakbeat was a simple discovery. As a DJ, Kool Herc watched the dancers closely to see what made them jump up and move; he found that the secret was in the breakbeat, the point in a song when the vocals cut out for a few seconds and the instruments and drums stand alone. Herc figured out that by taking two of the same records, he could cue up the breakbeat and switch back and forth between records, extending the break as much as he desired. "They always wanted to hear the breaks after breaks after breaks after breaks," recalled Herc in Jeff Chang's book *Can't Stop Won't Stop*. These extended breakbeats, which he called "the merry-go-round," began to take over his entire set and launched the trend in which "B-boys" would dance in a style that would later come to be called break dancing.

The parties grew in popularity along with the name of DJ Kool Herc. They went from backyards and rec rooms to city parks where power might be *borrowed* from a streetlight or maintenance shed. These public events could go all night and draw a crowd from all over the borough and often across gang lines. Herc required that peace be kept. "Listen. The first discrepancy, I'm pulling the plug. Let's get that straight right now," Herc said. "So anybody start anything, any disturbance or any discrepancy, any beef, I'm pulling the plug because I'm not going to be here for the repercussions." The audience was quick to agree, and people united around their love of dancing and music.

"It started coming together as far as the gangs terrorizing a lot of known discotheques back in the days," DJ Kool Herc said. "I had respect from a lot of the gang members because they used to go to school with me. I played what they liked and acknowledged their neighborhood when they came to my party. I was the people's choice. I was their investment. They made me who I am, and I never fronted on them. No matter how big my name got, I was always in the neighborhood."

Among those who witnessed a Kool Herc party was Jazzy Jay, a Zulu Nation B-boy and DJ. "Instead of gangs, they started turning into little area crews where they would do a little bit of dirt. In every area, there would be a DJ crew or a break-dance crew," explained Jay in *Can't Stop Won't Stop*. "Competition fueled the whole thing." The Universal Zulu Nation ultimately pulled members from rival gangs and turn into a social movement that promoted Afrocentric roots and included rappers and affiliates who would achieve later success (such as Q-Tip from a Tribe Called Quest).

Words, music, dance, and art replaced fists, guns, knives, chains, and bats. But when it came to emceeing, another element took root: the "D-Boy" (or "Dope Boy"). Dope Boy rap tells the story of hustling in the ghettos. It captures the lifestyle of a drug dealer, from a corner boy to a kingpin. The pioneers of this kind of "reality rap" were Grandmaster Flash and the Furious Five with their 1982 hit "The Message." The MCs rap about the woe of Bronx living—people pissing on the street, bill collectors, stickup kids in the park. It sounds quaint compared to the gangsta rap that would follow in the late '80s. The emergence of the crack era brought riches to the hood, but it also ratcheted up the violence. An AK-47 was the new switchblade. Inspired by the gangster lifestyle and gangbanging, this new style of hip-hop related what was going on in the streets. There were many hard-core gangsta rappers, but N.W.A. brought the genre to the mainstream. Then came the rappers who covered drug dealing and hustling.

"Our raps are documentary. We don't take sides," Ice Cube told *The Guardian* in 1989. "The parents, the police and the people of the local community are scared of what we say. We use the same kind of language as the kids use every day. In the Black community, the ministers and teachers don't deny that the problems we rap about exist, but they'd rather sweep it under the rug."

Rappers like Ice T defined the streets with his song "Colors" in 1988 and the witty wordplay of Kool G Rap and others set the standard. But there was one MC who came on the scene and took the hustling/drug-dealing/dope-boy angle to another level. His lyrics captured vividly what was going down in the streets. You had to think that he'd done what he was rapping about (or had at least been there and witnessed it firsthand). Even the hustlers, knee-deep in the drug game, stopped dead to listen to him.

Born on December 4, 1969, Shawn Corey Carter, aka "Jay-Z," grew up in the Bedford Stuyvesant section of Brooklyn in the Marcy Houses, a housing project built in the 1940s. The Marcy Houses consisted of twenty-seven six-story buildings. For Jay-Z and so many others, the Marcy projects offered little. People did what they could to get by. Not everyone survives that environment, and crime seems like a viable career option. Kids fall victim to the streets and the drug game thinking it's the only way out. As they say in the hood, "You can't knock the hustle." It's a self-serving mentality.

When Jay-Z was coming up in the late '80s and early '90s, the crack cocaine trade was in full effect. Everyone wanted to make a fast buck—not only to survive, but to get out of the hood. Often the ends justify the means, and the streets can be a hard taskmaster. Jay-Z gained knowledge on the blocks that spawned him.

"That whole crack era, the Reagan years, it was everywhere," Jay-Z told *Vanity Fair* in 2013. "It just engulfed you. And crack was everywhere—it was inescapable. There wasn't any place you could go for isolation or a break. You go in the hallway; [there are] crackheads in the hallway. You look out in the puddles on the curbs—crack vials are littered in the side of the curbs. You could smell it in the hallways, that putrid smell; I can't explain it, but it's still in my mind when I think about it."

When you have nothing and you watch TV and look at magazines, you see high-end designer clothes, expensive cars and jewelry, big houses with long driveways—these *Robb Report* dreams—you want that life for yourself. You grow tired of your stomach growling, going to bed every night hungry, the pissy-smelling hallways, the elevators never working, and being all cramped up in these housing projects. It's a bleak reality for a kid, and anything seems better than where they're at.

You want better but can't find a job that will take you out of this everyday misery. Generations of families lived in the projects for decades. Families started more families. Couples meet each other in the same housing project or ones nearby. They have kids and stay in the projects. It's a cycle that continues for generations and makes people feel like that's where they belong.

And who wouldn't want to break that cycle, change their lives? Society talks about getting an education and then a job in the corporate world—but that's all an illusion. The system isn't set up for people from Marcy Houses. Look where these people came from. Their lives were designed for failure from the jump. It's what we've come to know as systemic oppression.

The information fed to minorities in public schools was preparing them for the wage-slavery pipeline. Many saw it coming. So a whole generation of young Black and Latino males rode the wave of the crack cocaine epidemic and became drug dealers. Some made progress, but too many became pawns in the game—getting sent to prison, succumbing to drug use, or even getting killed. Either way, you can say they were addicted to an illusion. Those who made a name for themselves or even made headlines playing this game may not have won in the end, but they left stories for others to tell. And Shawn Carter had a gift for telling them.

Like many Black males growing up in the hood, Shawn wanted the best shoes and clothes and everything else kids his age wanted. But money was tight—he was raised by a single mother who worked hard to provide for him, his brother Eric, and his two sisters. To make extra money, Shawn did odd jobs, but that didn't cut it in the hood. Other guys were wearing expensive sneakers, name-brand clothes, and jewelry. McDonald's or Kentucky Fried Chicken couldn't keep you fresh like that. So, like others, Shawn got involved in the drug game. A young hustler getting it by any means necessary.

"We were living in a tough situation, but my mother managed; she juggled. Sometimes we'd pay the light bill, sometimes we paid the phone, sometimes the gas went off. We weren't starving—we were eating, we were OK," Jay told *Vanity Fair*. "But it was things like you didn't want to be embarrassed when you went to school; you didn't want to have dirty sneakers or wear the same clothes over again." Being poor could be devastating for a kid.

Jay always had that thing for rhyming. He was just good with words. It was just in him. He was always banging beats on the table, reciting verses, or spitting freestyles. It was just a pastime or hobby to him at the time. He was serious, but not that serious. He just didn't see a future in it, never saw himself becoming a hip-hop star. Things like that weren't on his mind. He was hustling crack, trying to get to the money. Pursuing his American dream despite what might come.

One of the first dudes to turn Jay on to hustling was a guy named DeHaven Irby. DeHaven schooled Jay and showed him the ins and outs of the crack game on the low level, the hand-to-hand drug-dealer side. They even went out to New Jersey to distribute crack vials. When hustlers from New York City took their "work" out of town, they usually made double what they made back in the five boroughs. Street legend holds that DeHaven and Jay were getting money.

Jay attended George Westinghouse High School in Brooklyn. Christopher "Biggie Smalls" Wallace and Trevor "Busta Rhymes" Smith went there too. Hip-hop lore says that Jay and Busta battled each other way back then and that Jay demolished Busta easily. Battling was how Jay made a name for himself when it came to spitting. Jay got with another spitter from around the Marcy Houses, someone who was more seasoned and had major stature in Brooklyn and in the streets. His name was Jonathan Burks, but he was known as "Jaz" or "Jaz-O." Jaz was five years older, so he took Jay under his wing, showing him how to properly construct songs.

"I connected with an older kid who had a reputation as the best rapper in Marcy," Jay wrote in his 2010 book *Decoded*. "Jaz was his name— and we started practicing our rhymes into a heavy-ass tape recorder with a makeshift mic attached." Jaz-O took Jay to studio sessions, showed him how tracks were laid, showed him the sound booths and how everything was done. He gave the young hustler a view into the hip-hop world he'd never had before. He showed him a way that was different from the streets. Jay absorbed it all and was a quick learner.

At the same time, Jay was also getting schooled in the art of the drug game by the infamous street legend Calvin "Klein" Bacote. His nickname came from the fashion designer. Bacote was a fan and wore the designer threads religiously, flaunting his wealth around the hood. "Klein" was definitely that dude in the crack trade in Brooklyn. A true don of the block. A gangster's gangsta.

Bacote was a high-level dealer who supplied mid-to-high-level dealers and later expanded his business out of state, where drug profits tripled and, in some places, quadrupled compared to New York. He had a multi-state operation. His team was getting so much money in the "DMV" (DC, Maryland, and Virginia), they were living the extravagant life of Pablo Escobar. Young thugs on the come up.

To the young hustler Jay, "Klein" was that guy, and Jay started running with him and his team. He wanted to be like Klein. He was the epitome of the New York City street hustler, and Jay saw himself following in his footsteps. Jay was now caught between the music game and the drug hustle, enjoying both sides to the fullest. A player in the streets and in the rap game. Someone who had options on two different fronts.

Jaz-O now had a record deal with EMI and came out with two albums. In 1989, he released *Word to the Jaz* and his second LP, *To Your Soul*, came out a year later. It wasn't like he had a promising career, but he was making it out of the ghetto, and, unlike the drug game, he wasn't risking jail being involved in the music business. He wasn't falling into the trap.

"Jaz-O had it going on," Calvin Klein Bacote said in an interview with Mike Trampe. "Jay just actually took a ride with it, but I think that probably was the best thing for Jay for him to kinda like get an understanding of what the industry was about and things of that nature. But at that time when Jaz-O came out, Jay wasn't ready for that moment. His moment came when his actual time was. Jaz-O was just trying to keep Jay away from the streets and have him more caught up into the music thing."

Jay-Z took on the role of hype man, performing on stage with Jaz-O, vibing with the crowd, learning how to control the audience, getting a real feel for performing. He did two studio songs that made it onto Jaz's albums. Now Jay was actually an established MC, who rhymed on records that were getting spins on the radio. His stature was rising. Maybe he had a future in this.

Jaz and Jay did songs together like "Hawaiian Sophie." Jay was featured in that music video. He was also on "The Originators," which came out in 1990. Jay had a fast-paced, Das EFX style when he rapped back then. He ended up going on tour with Jaz and DJ Irv from Queens. As he traveled the country with them, he got a taste of the performing life. Jay and Jaz did shows with the rap group Main Source. This is how Jay met a younger MC and protege from Queensbridge who went by the name of "Nasty Nas."

Jay was still in the streets hustling part-time. It wasn't like he was really eating off of the rap-music shit. He wasn't emceeing full-time; the streets had more of a hold on him, so he was leaning more into hustling. Jay wanted to get money, and the drug game was where it was at. Money talked and Jay was trying to get paid.

"I started out as a really small guy on the street, but after a while I did OK and that made it even harder to leave," Jay told *GQ* in 2005. "I felt like I was making even more than the rappers. I had a Lexus with TVs in the car. I felt like my life was better than theirs. You mighta had a rope chain but so did I."

At this time in Jay's life, his partner Calvin Klein was wanted by the DEA and his operation was under surveillance. Everything was coming to a head for Klein, and Jay was starting to spit that drug talk in his raps.

There was no doubt that he was there in the mix of all the street shit, but only some know to what extent. As Jay's career advanced, people have often wondered how deep he was in the game.

It was known that Calvin Klein's name rang bells; he was that dude and Jay was with him so that's why the accounts that Jay rapped about have always been realistic and believable. In 1989, Calvin "Klein" Bacote and Shawn "Jay-Z" Carter were arrested and taken into custody in Maryland. They were held on charges of attempted murder and assault with a deadly weapon; they both faced up to forty years in prison.

It was said that Jay—out of loyalty to his friend Klein—was willing to take the charges, but Klein wouldn't allow it. Klein paid lawyers over fifty thousand dollars to get Jay off the case. At trial, Jay was Klein's character witness, testified on his behalf. Klein was still found guilty of a lesser charge and sentenced to four years in prison.

"Jay and I wound up [getting] caught," Klein told VladTV. "We actually got locked up, charged with [attempted] murder, [attempted] murder to maim, battery, assault, possession of a deadly weapon. Jay was like, 'Yo, Klein, you been through a lot, I don't really have no record, I could take the weight of the case.' I kinda thought of the man's career. I didn't want him to miss that opportunity."

In the fed case Klein was charged with conspiracy to distribute cocaine and pleaded out and was sentenced to 261 months. After several appeals, that sentence was later reduced to 188 months. Klein completed thirteen years on that sentence. Jay continued spitting pieces and bits of his hustling days. How much of it was really true? Who knows—it was his story, and he could tell it how he wanted—but the real players give Jay his props.

"One thing that I never wanted to do while I was in there was have a phone conversation with Jay," Klein said. "I didn't want to even have any type of association with him in no kinda way to kinda put him in a bad situations or any type of harm or anything of that nature."

Some critics have questioned Jay's street cred, but vouching for him you have Jaz, who put Jay on in the rap game and knew that Jay was into the streets; DeHaven Irby, who introduced Jay to the game and has verified his involvement; Calvin Klein, who Jay ran with and who was a certified street legend and has talked about his past with Jay Z; and DJ Irv, who remembered Jay pulling up in luxurious cars with TVs in the headrest in the early to mid-'90s before his rap career blew up. Many witnessed Jay's exploits.

You also have cats in the federal prison system who will say that Jay was in the mix. Marcy projects kingpin Stanley "The Man" Burrell—who was hit with a "continuing criminal enterprise" charge, which is one of the most serious kingpin drug charges—knew Jay when he was in the streets. There's also Theodore "T. J." Henderson, another kingpin from Marcy projects, and Emory "Vegas" Jones, a known hustler who did fed time and who's still a close friend to Jay. They can all give their accounts and verify Jay's legitimacy in the streets.

Most cats in the game looked at the drug-dealing lifestyle in the '80s and '90s fondly, but there were more negatives than positives. No one really ever pointed out the consequences and factors that outweighed the glamor of the money. First, you are taking chances in a game where there are no real winners. Selling drugs is illegal. You can lose your life and your freedom. No one is rapping about that. An accurate picture isn't always portrayed.

What's more, you can't really trust anyone, even family members will snake you in this game. You have to keep an eye out for the police, the stickup kids, family members get kidnapped, you are always in constant danger. No one speaks about this; they're usually too busy flossing and showing off what they obtained. But it can all be lost at any moment.

As for your suppliers, you can't trust them either. They might sell you some bad work that you can't get rid of or snitch on you and set you up when they catch a case. It's an up-and-down game of chance with traps everywhere. Anyone can be the police or an enemy posing as a friend. You're in constant fear as you're trying to enjoy the life and justify it, if only for a few seconds. Dudes will trade everything for one moment on top.

The drug game is not a promising career. It doesn't come with life or health insurance, retirement or pension plans. There is way more to lose than there is to gain. That's just the reality of it all, and no one raps about that. Only the accolades are lauded in verse and held up to the masses. The real story is often left untold—the generations of Black youth who have lost their lives or spent decades in prison.

Listening to Jay's earlier work, in the lyrics on his first album, *Reasonable Doubt*, he points out escaping secret indictments, being under scrutiny of the feds, losing close friends and associates to prison, and even death. He speaks about escaping shots that were aimed at and meant for him. A harrowing existence.

Somewhere in his drug career he realized it was time to exit and take a different path. It was the best decision he ever made. He speaks about coming into the rap game with $100,000 on stash. His ties to the crack trade were apparent. He was definitely a player despite what his detractors said. You can see it too in his ties to partners Damon Dash and Kareem "Biggs" Burke and the Roc-A-Fella Records deal. The dream team that launched Jay's career, "Dame" and "Biggs," both had ties to the streets that came from hustling, and Biggs eventually did time because of his hustling connections.

After creating the beat for hip-hop, DJ Kool Herc moved from public, all-ages parties to the Savoy Manor nightclub at 149th Street and Grand Concourse. It was a joint venture with a fan, Aaron O'Bryant, who was ready to move from drug dealer to party promoter once the Bronx Youth Gang Task Force started cracking skulls left and right. But audiences began declining, and Herc found himself more and more on the sidelines as new up-and-comers emerged. Bronx DJs like Grandmaster Flash took Herc's "merry-go-round" and brought it to a science with his analytic turntable theory, and Grand Wizzard Theodore built on Flash's turntable science and invented record scratching. After Herc got stabbed one night after leaving the club, he decided to step aside and leave the rap foundation he helped cement for the younger guys to build on.

In Boogie Down Productions' "The Bridge Is Over," KRS-One rhymed that *Brooklyn keeps taking it / The Bronx keeps creating it.* The style set down in the Bronx spread to the other boroughs and from there the world. In crime and hip-hop, there are those who pave the way for others to take things to the next level. There would be no Lucky Luciano without an Arnold Rothstein before him. Jay-Z took the foundation set with gangsta rap and brought it to a new level of mainstream popularity. Whereas Ice Cube once advertised for St. Ides Malt Liquor, Jay-Z launched his own vodka brand, Armand de Brignac. His business ventures varied from a fashion label, a cannabis company, to investments in new tech like Uber. In the streets the hustlers' dream was always to become a legitimate businessman and Jay Z did exactly that—no bullets, no jail, only one success after another for hip-hop's Brooklyn Don.

THE TRIALS AND TRIBULATIONS OF MAC DRE

SF

Thizz Entertainment and Mac Dre

7

"MAC DRE'S THIZZ ENTERTAINMENT IMPLICATED in Ecstasy Ring," announced a *BET* headline in 2012. Court records showed that more than twenty-five affiliates of the Bay Area record label, Thizz Entertainment, founded by Mac Dre, were arrested. During the investigation, agents seized approximately forty-five thousand MDMA pills, four pounds of crack cocaine, a half-pound of heroin, and $200,000 in suspected drug money. In the parlance of the streets, Mac Dre was balling.

"This is another example of the partnership that exists between the Drug Enforcement Administration and the Vallejo Police Department to improve the safety of our community and reduce the level of violence associated with drug dealing," said Vallejo Police Chief Robert Nichelini. "We appreciate the efforts of the U.S. Attorney for the Eastern District of California in coordinating the investigation and prosecuting the persons involved in such a complex and dangerous criminal enterprise."

According to the criminal complaint, the DEA-led investigation uncovered a network of drug distributors working in the Crest neighborhood of Vallejo, along with individuals who transported large quantities of drugs outside of California to make a larger profit. Several subjects of the investigation were rappers signed to Thizz Entertainment. The origin of the label traced back to the notorious Vallejo-based robbery crews known as the "Romper Room Gang."

The Romper Room Gang was named after a children's show on public television, but their antics weren't child's play. These dudes were *getting it*, plain and simple. The crew specialized in armed bank robberies, drug trafficking, and murder and were active throughout the late '80s and '90s. But as a result of Vallejo police investigations, with the assistance from federal law enforcement, aka "the alphabet boys," many members of the gang were convicted of federal crimes and incarcerated for several years in the state and federal prison systems. *If you're going to do the crime, you have to be willing to do the time.*

The complaint also said that Thizz Entertainment started in 1999 as a record label to produce and promote rappers from the Bay Area, mainly from the Crest neighborhood. The name Thizz Entertainment originates from the term "thizz," which is slang for the drug MDMA, also known as "ecstasy." In many songs by Thizz artists, the lyrics glorify and promote the use and distribution of MDMA pills. Rolling on "Molly" was a thing in hip-hop circles even back in the late '90s. The complaint also alleged that the targets of the investigation engaged in large-scale drug trafficking while they were releasing rap albums for Thizz. Dudes were gangsta rappers for real. Ain't no faking it.

"They were all rap artists first, they had some pretty big names on that label," Sacramento County Sheriff's Detective Brad Rose, who helped crack the case, told *NPR*. "But those drugs are highly profitable." During the conspiracy, agents uncovered trafficking of MDMA, cocaine, cocaine base, heroin, oxycodone, and marijuana, in violation of federal law. The complaint detailed drug shipments sent from the Vallejo area to Oklahoma City; Jamaica, Queens, New York; Atlanta; and Milwaukee. The Romper Room Gang was a national outfit.

"This story right here starts out kinda ill because when Gucci was telling me about this cat, he was really into it," former street general Shakim Bio said. "It felt like he was adding in a little extra shit-talking. Gucci was from South Jamaica, Queens, in New York City. He was the typical Jamaica, Queens cat—thought he was fly, making moves that everyone else wanted to. That's Queens cats for you. They think they're smoother than everyone in the room. Always outthinking shit that they outwit themselves."

Gucci was doing a twenty-year federal bid for outwitting himself. He forgot that when he was heading back to New York from Miami that he left his HK (Heckler & Koch) 10 mm handgun in his luggage. He put his luggage through the carry-on scanner only to be carried on to prison, and then the feds came to see him months later after one of his shipments got caught up. He was locked up so Gucci didn't get the chance to pick up the shipment, but the charges picked him up. He took the twenty years.

"He was in USP Lompoc, when it was a penitentiary," Shakim Bio said. "It's a medium-status joint now, but when it was a penitentiary, shit was real. Everything was serious. So seeing Gucci all laid-back telling me about this San Francisco cat who can spit, I half-assed listened to him talking because Gucci likes to stretch out stories a little. Gucci put it like 'this dude is lyrically insane with the verbals.' His name was Mac Dre."

Shakim wasn't really listening until Gucci mentioned that this dude Mac Dre was so nice that when he went home Prince from the Supreme Team, who was at USP Lompoc at the time, stamped Mac Dre as being "Super Official" to the point that one of Mac Dre's tracks was featured on Black Hand Entertainment's *Black Gangster* movie soundtrack—the film based on Donald Goines's book that Supreme was making before he went back to prison.

Mac Dre was born Andre Louis Hicks on July 5, 1970, in Oakland, California, but moved to the Vallejo area in the late '90s. He would often frequent the Country Club Crest neighborhood. Mac Dre began rapping in the early '80s and used the stage name "MC Dre" in 1984 but altered it to "Mac Dre" in 1985 because he felt the "MC Dre" name sounded too much like an East Coast rap artist. He dropped the single "Too Hard for the Fuckin' Radio," which was as much of an introduction as it was a mission statement.

Throughout his career, Mac Dre remained fiercely independent and found success without major-label distribution or national radio play. "Thizz [Dre] just seemed like he was made to be independent," said Oakland rapper Too Short. His first label was called Romp Records, a nod to the Romper Room Crew that he and his friends ran with, which represented the kind of art-imitates-life moment that permeates hip-hop.

While Dre focused on his music, his "cuddies" (best friends) had other interests—they were all about robbing.

"My crew, like any other crew, somebody gonna come up with an idea, and as youngsters—teenagers—sometimes you try shit," said J-Digg, a member of the Romper Room Crew, in an interview with VladTV. "So that's what we did. One of the dudes had an idea, 'Man, let's do this. I gotta *lick*, a *sweet*, an inside job [at a Pizza Parlor] kind of shit. And the first one worked."

The Romper Room pizza-parlor heists around the Bay Area ended up on a 1992 episode of *Unsolved Mysteries*. Meanwhile the teenagers graduated from robbing mom-and-pop pizza shops to robbing banks. They were from the school of hard knocks and making progress meant bigger licks.

While Mac Dre did work in the streets like dealing dope, the Romper Room didn't allow him to participate in the crew's heists. "When the pizza robberies were effective, he had his single out ["Too Hard for the Fuckin' Radio"] so the thing was to keep Dre out the way," said J-Digg. "You are the rapper. You stay out the way. Let us do this street shit. My nigga, you just get us to the top with this rap shit."

The thousands of dollars funneling into the crew from the robberies would be used to buy Mac Dre recording equipment, keyboards, microphones, and anything else he thought he needed to tackle the rap game. But despite the Romper Room's attempts to keep Dre away from the robberies, he would nevertheless get attention from local law enforcement.

NPR reported that some of Mac Dre's songs, released through his label Romp Records, implicated him in a series of robberies associated with the Crest's Romper Room Gang. In one song Mac Dre depicted a credit-union robbery in vivid detail. He was taking the reality-rap angle that N.W.A. made infamous to the extreme. While N.W.A. blatantly shouted "fuck the police," Mac Dre named-dropped and taunted the detective hounding him about these robberies. He was all the way live. He dedicated "Punk Police" to Vallejo Police Detective Dave McGraw, rapping, *Punk police with a one-track mind / Man, you can't even find who's been robbin' you blind.*

With gangsta rap blowing up and Mac Dre being so out front with it, law enforcement officials began to dissect his lyrics, along with those of other local rappers, to see if they could piece together crimes and use Mac Dre's lyrics as evidence. "They were bragging about it on a rap CD," Lieutenant JoAnn West said at a Vallejo Police Department news conference at the time. "It's kind of brazen for them to brag about it as though they were untouchable." But that was hip-hop—up front and in your face.

On March 26, 1992, at the age of twenty-one, Mac Dre was surrounded by the FBI and Fresno and Vallejo police. Police stated that Dre and his friends had allegedly cased a bank that they planned to rob but changed their minds when they saw a local Fresno TV news van in the bank's parking lot. When police questioned Dre, he said that he didn't know anything. They subsequently charged him with conspiracy to commit bank robbery, though one hadn't occurred. The feds play dirty when it comes down to it. Crime or no crime, it's all the same.

Mac Dre's friends said he had nothing to do with the robberies, but in the feds' eyes he was guilty by association and because of his rap lyrics. "We always have been a neighborhood where we get down with each other. We come from a city that has nothing," Jamal Rocker, a Vallejo rapper known as "Mac Mall" and a contemporary of Mac Dre, told NPR. "Like, when you hear the word 'cuddie,' it means cousin and friend. Even 'cutthroat'—that's a term of endearment."

Mac Dre was sentenced to five years in federal prison after he refused a plea deal for the conspiracy charge. Even though he had nothing to do with the crimes, he refused to snitch on his crew. He proceeded to trial and was convicted. It was during this federal prison bid that he started writing more, perfecting his craft as a songwriter. He even recorded in prison and developed a business plan with his mother. This is how Gucci heard about him—through the prison grapevine.

Mac Dre did four years out of that sentence and learned to appreciate the nuances of the free world and reinterpret what fun was all about. Upon his release from USP Lompoc, Mac Dre decided that he wanted to start doing music that people could dance to and moved away from gangsta rap and Romp Records. He had love from the streets and a rep from his prison bid—the Bay Area was ready to embrace whatever he was ready to do. He founded a new label, Thizz Entertainment (with Romper Room member Kilo Kurt) and was managed by his mother.

This new sound would become influential in the development of the Bay Area's "hyphy movement," a regional hip-hop style that featured electro hooks, big beats, and party lyrics. It was just at home in a rave club as it was on "sideshows" of illegal car maneuvers like ghost riding, donuts, and street racing. "He captured people's imagination, and he symbolized a music era," said Bay Area activist and hip-hop journalist Davey D in the documentary *Mac Dre: Legend of the Bay.*

As his popularity grew, other areas took notice, and Mac Dre began performing all along the West Coast and into the Midwest. It seemed that his dream of going national was finally in reach. After a Kansas City show, however, tragedy struck. An unidentified gunman shot up the group's van as it traveled on Interstate 70 back to the hotel. Mac Dre died from a bullet to the neck. It was hard to believe because Kansas City had so much love for him. There were rumors in the street about who killed him, with some pointing the finger at KC rapper Fat Tone, a claim that J-Digg dismisses.

"The hardest thing to me about him getting killed when he did, was that he was right at the cusp of really being the next major rapper in the business," said Dre's mother, Wanda Salvatto, in the documentary *Mac Dre: Legend of the Bay*. "It got cut short then and there. That's the thing that hurt the most."

Eight years after his death, police targeted Mac Dre again, even though he was dead. When the federal indictments came out for the ecstasy ring, the names Mac Dre and Thizz Entertainment were everywhere. But despite the hoopla and incriminating press reports, Mac Dre's mom refuted the claims made by the police. "Thizz Entertainment is actually me. There are no artists signed to the label," Salvatto, who wasn't mentioned or charged in the investigation, told the San Jose *Mercury News* "I worked very hard to clean up and maintain a legitimate label and business for my son. I don't want to confuse what we do with our fans."

Mac Dre would have been proud. He'll be remembered as a certified G and hip-hop icon who tried to make a better life for himself but was gunned down in the process like so many before him.

GANGSTER
TURNED MUSIC
MOGUL

BK

Czar

Entertainment

and

Enemy Henchman

8

ON NOVEMBER 30, 1994, TUPAC SHAKUR was beaten, shot, and robbed outside of Quad Recording Studios in Manhattan. He lived to tell the tale and show the bullet holes as the high-profile incident made headlines, both in hip-hop journalism and the mainstream media. The fallout would cause the East Coast–West Coast rap beefs to spiral into all-out war. The question everybody was asking, including Tupac himself, was who had set him up? From the streets to the pages of the *Los Angeles Times* to the lyrics of Tupac's songs, one name kept coming up—Jimmy Henchman.

James "Jimmy Henchman" Rosemond was born on February 5, 1965, in Harlem to two Haitian immigrants. He grew up in Flatbush, Brooklyn, in the Vanderveer Estates housing projects. During his youth he was known as "Jimmy Ace." Even though he was a Haitian dude, many mistook him for Jamaican—to the locals all the island guys were the same. He could hang out with Caribbean dudes heavy but also ran the streets with the sheisty Brooklyn thugs. Rosemond was in the middle of it all— hustling, robbing, and networking with crooks from all over Brooklyn. A true thug in every sense of the word.

"My parents migrated from Haiti in the 1960s to escape the iron fist of Papa Doc," Rosemond told *Don Diva Magazine*. "My parents divorced when I was young and my mother was left to raise five children alone. She couldn't keep up with me. Since she had two jobs, I was left unsupervised most of the time." And with little or no parental guidance, the young Rosemond gravitated to the streets to find love and acceptance there.

Street love caught up with Rosemond at the young age of sixteen. A bicycle theft left him incarcerated in a juvenile unit in Rikers Island where he connected with others who would grow up to become street legends and hustlers. These connections led "Jimmy Ace" to get an advanced degree in hustling and criminology and become known and associated with the likes of King Tut, Scooter, Haitian Jack, Baby Sam, Homicide, Brian Glaze, and other Brooklyn thugs.

In jail and on the outside, Jimmy Ace seemed like the typical quiet dude, but he was always scheming. He worked behind the scenes and was a networker who had associates in many circles. Being able to move in the Caribbean crowd plus blend in with the Brooklyn dudes was a skill that helped him survive both on the streets and while locked up. He was smarter than most of the gun thugs he associated with and had no trouble outwitting them. He got into graffiti early on, a natural B-boy who moved with the dope boys. That was how he first made his name in the streets— literally—as he scrawled his handle wherever he could.

"In my early days I was with a crew called the 'Untouchables,'" Rosemond told *Don Diva Magazine*. "I was the only Haitian in the crew; everyone else was Jamaican. I used the tag 'Ace One' and that was my handle. I would hit train yards, buses, and hallways. My handle would later evolve into 'Jimmy Ace.' I wanted to make a name for myself. I would say my name with a bit of James Bond flair to it while holding a .45 caliber. I would say, 'My name is Ace, Jimmy Ace.'" He was like Jimmy Cliff in *The Harder They Come*, the picture of a Wild West Jamaican outlaw, strutting to the rude-boy beat. Gangsta to the core.

The Jamaicans not only exposed a young Rosemond to street life, but musically he felt connected to the Caribbean reggae/dancehall scene. The rhyming melodies and big beats in the Jamaican rude-boy scene aren't that far removed from what would become hip-hop. Godfather of hip-hop DJ Kool Herc got his start spinning reggae tracks before he switched to break-beats pulled from funk, R&B, and soul. There were different elements of the rude-boy style, and artists like Shinehead, Ninjaman, Nicodemus, Shelly Thunder, and Yellowman represented. Later Shabba Ranks became a superstar in this genre and took over the airwaves with the ferocity and bravado that this style epitomized. The Jamaican gangs represented the rude-boy lifestyle, and Jimmy Ace was heavy among them.

His main crew was the Touchies, a vicious Jamaican gang that took no shorts. As a high school dropout, Rosemond turned his attention to making his rep shout out as widely as his graffiti tags had throughout the borough. It was about having your name ring bells. But his rise was hindered by one gun charge after another that put him in and out of jail—a story that repeated throughout his career.

While in prison, Rosemond got his GED and later enrolled in college. He was smart enough to know that he needed an education. When he made parole, he left with an associate's degree. Coming home in 1988 at the age of twenty-three during the crack cocaine boom, Jimmy Ace fell right into hustling. College or not he still was going to do him and get money—by doing what he knew best and using his intelligence and leadership skills. He also expanded his connections from mostly Jamaicans to gangsters from all over the five boroughs and New York State.

In 1991, soon-to-be-star R. Kelly was being managed by David Hyatt, a Jamaican and close associate of Jimmy Ace. Dave brought Jimmy Ace into the music industry. The music industry was a new frontier where street dudes could blend in and make moves among the celebrities and go unnoticed. Every rap artist needed a wolf to represent for them when the shit jumped off. It was a scene in which street smarts and connections could help a guy like Jimmy make power moves in a legitimate arena. The industry money even rivaled the fortune you could make running drugs. Jimmy had found his niche.

In 1992, Jimmy got a chance with a few other associates to throw a birthday bash for Fab Five Freddie, who was hosting the show *Yo MTV Raps!* at the time. Freddie was an icon in the hip-hop world and had tremendous connections—ones that Jimmy Henchman needed if he wanted to make his move into hip-hop permanent. The savvy hustler made sure the guest list was filled with publicists, rap journalists, and music-industry executives.

"It brought other people from MTV," said Rosemond in an interview with *BLOW!* magazine. "From there we end up doing the 'How Can I Be Down' conference. From there I went on to become a manager for producers. My first hit was 'Shoop' for Salt-N-Pepa. The rest was really history." Jimmy knew what angles he had to work to make a career in music. He had conquered the streets and hip-hop was next.

In those days the "How Can I Be Down" music-conference convention was where people seeking to get into the music industry could get their music heard and could meet, network, and party with music record execs, producers, A&Rs, and publicists without getting the runaround. Rosemond removed the gatekeeper dynamic. He was a DIY guy at heart and wanted others to be able to get into the industry like he had. No one had ever done this. Rosemond proved himself not only a player in the rap game but also an innovator.

"The industry was a whole new world for me," Rosemond told *Don Diva*. "No one knew me from being in the street. People stopped calling me Jimmy Ace and started calling me Jimmy Henchman after the company I created, Henchmen Productions." Even with the new career and name change, Rosemond was still the same Brooklyn dude who was grimy and playing chess in the streets, just now on a higher level. He knew there were *levels to this shit* long before Meek Mill rapped about it.

Unaware that the FBI was looking for him because of a drug charge in North Carolina, Rosemond continued to build his brand. He believed he was now insulated from the streets. He signed an R&B duo named Groove Theory made up of beatmaker/producer Bryce Wilson (from the rap group Mantronix) and singer-songwriter and keyboardist Amel Eliza Larrieux. He secured a deal with Sony Music Group and executive-produced their debut album under Henchmen/Epic Records. Their single "Tell Me" reached number 5 on the Billboard charts, and the album would go on to be certified gold. It appeared that Rosemond had broken into the music game. He was generating real money, had a viable production company, and had hit songs on the charts. But his past came back. He got arrested for possession of a firearm in midtown Manhattan—just like a common thug.

When he got printed in New York, the outstanding North Carolina charge popped up, but luckily Jimmy dodged the detainer and made bond. The rumor was that someone in jail had changed his bond from $100,000 to $1,000 and he was able to get the fuck out of there. Even with the law bearing down on him, Jimmy continued to work to establish himself in the hip-hop world. He managed some of rap's biggest artists and consulted with record labels like Interscope, Motown, and Virgin. He also made inroads with other street gangsters moving in similar circles.

Jimmy Henchman still had heavy street connections who were major players in the hustling game. Real street thugs. One was Jacques Agnant, better known as "Haitian Jack." Haitian Jack was a big-time gangster in the New York underworld and had befriended up-and-coming star Tupac Shakur. A lot of rappers talk about their affiliations, but Tupac was running with real street dudes. That's part of the allure of Tupac but also what led to his downfall.

Rosemond remembers taking Tupac on a guided tour of New York's toughest neighborhoods while the young rapper and actor was shooting the film *Above the Rim*. In many ways Tupac wanted to be seen as a peer of the street legends and learn the inside details of the dope game. In many ways he was getting into character for his film roles and getting material for his rhymes.

"I showed him from example. I brought him to Brooklyn with me," said Rosemond, in Ethan Brown's book *Queens Reigns Supreme*. "We were up with dreads in houses full of weed, full of guns, full of money. It was, '*This is how we do it.*' " But Tupac's wild behavior, such as carrying a loaded weapon while Rosemond was driving, annoyed Rosemond. Pac seemed to want to live the character he portrayed in *Juice* and didn't know how to play it safe. A reckless artist clamoring for the streets.

More trouble followed when Tupac accompanied love-interest Madonna and Haitian Jack club-hopping and was said to have been involved in a gang rape of a nineteen-year-old woman. Ayanna Jackson claimed that Haitian Jack, Tupac, and others had sexually assaulted her in a hotel room. "Tupac was lying on the couch," she said in an interview with VladTV, "In my mind I'm thinking, *This motherfucker just raped me, and he's lying up here like a king acting as if nothing happened.*" Tupac dismissed the accusations in a *New York Daily News* article, blaming Haitian Jack and other "hangers-on" and claiming that he had not participated. Rosemond was furious and confronted Tupac about discussing the case with the tabloids and dissing the New York hustlers who had welcomed the rapper.

Street life is much different and more real than rap diss tracks. On November 30, 1994, the twenty-two-year-old Shakur, who was awaiting the verdict of the sexual assault trial, was contacted by associates of Henchmen Productions to do a record with Brooklyn rapper Little Shawn at the Quad Recording Studios in Times Square. Shakur was offered $7,000 in cash to lay down a few verses on a track. Even though their relationship was strained, Tupac still had gratitude for what Henchman had done for him and accepted the offer. Plagued by legal fees, he also needed the money.

When Shakur and his three-man entourage arrived late at the studio, they were ambushed by two armed men in army fatigues. The focus of the assault was on Shakur, who was pistol-whipped, robbed of $40,000 worth of jewelry, and allegedly shot five times, including once to the groin. Shakur claimed the bullets came from the assailants, but others suggested that Tupac shot himself while trying to pull a gun concealed in his pants. While this was going on, upstairs were several prominent New York rappers, producers, and music executives, including Jimmy Henchman.

Henchman was accused of orchestrating the attack. This was the event that triggered the East Coast–West Coast rap war that cost the lives of many and led to the deaths of both the Notorious B.I.G. (aka Biggie Smalls) and Tupac Shakur. Before it was just diss records and occasional fistfights between crews. The shooting took it to a new level, and the hip-hop murders that followed still haven't been solved. Henchman was fingered fifteen years later by one of the assailants, Dexter Isaac, who claimed he was paid to rob and shoot Tupac by Henchman. Henchman denied it.

While on tour in Los Angeles with his Groovy Theory duo, Henchman once again got popped for gun charges. At the time his production company had several hits, including Toni Braxton's number-1 Billboard Hot 100 single, "You're Making Me High." The case in North Carolina was deep, but not even the feds could slap drug-statute charges that would stick to Henchman. He was somehow able to get the gun charges in New York suppressed at a hearing and pled guilty to time served on bail jumping. Henchman was then extradited to Los Angeles to face the gun charges he caught there. Rosemond took a plea and got five years, which he served at FCI Otisville. Again, his prison time offered networking opportunities. He met Brian McCleod and enlisted him to help keep his street activities alive and continue making moves in the music industry.

Rosemond returned home in 2001 with a reputation on the streets, in prison, and in the music industry as being a man who made shit happen. But he also established a reputation as a true hip-hop gangster. In a *Vibe* article about the Tupac shooting, Pac called Rosemond an "omnipotent gangster." The author of the article claimed that "Henchman became an übervillain not just to Tupac fans but also to the hip-hop world at large." Rosemond was being likened to other infamous thug moguls like Death Row's Suge Knight. "If you talked to people on the East Coast, my name would come up. If you talked to people on the West Coast, Suge's name would come up," Henchman said in the documentary series *Unjust Justice*.

With some shying away from dealing with him, Rosemond started to distance himself from his street connections. Henchmen Productions was renamed Czar Entertainment. Rosemond continued to establish himself as a serious player in the media, music, and even movies. He was the executive producer of several albums and movie soundtracks, including *Bullet Proof Love, Volume 1,* a compilation album featuring artists Memphis, Bleek, and Prodigy; Sharissa's debut album *No Half Steppin* on Henchmen/Motown; the soundtracks for *Romeo Must Die,* starring Jet Li and the late Aaliyah, with the rapper DMX and others featured; and the soundtrack for the movie *Exit Wound.* Henchman was straight business in the corporate world and negotiated deals worth millions, and he pushed into other legitimate businesses such as opening a burger franchise with Queen Latifa.

Henchman continued to work in music and movies. He executive-produced the films *Belly 2, The Millionaire Boys Club, The Cookout 2,* and the VIBE Music Awards. His management clients included Sean Kingston, Wyclef, Akon, Pleasure P, Gorilla Black, and Brandy. He even branched out into athletics, managing Haitian American boxer Andre Berto and Mike Tyson, and negotiated Tyson's 2002 megafight with world heavyweight champion Lennox Lewis

Henchman also kept active politically and philanthropically. In 2003, he joined the movement led by Russell Simmons to overturn the New York State Rockefeller Drug Laws. He rallied at City Hall with other celebrities to campaign against the harsh drug laws. He was also among a group of entertainment managers who were asked in 2007 by Barack Obama's campaign team to help secure votes for Obama's first run for the presidency. In appreciation for his efforts, Henchman was invited as a special guest to President Obama's first inauguration on January 20, 2009. In 2010, Rosemond executive-produced BET's *S.O.S. Saving Ourselves: Help for Haiti* along with Mona Scott and others. It was a telethon that raised money for the victims of the deadly earthquakes in Haiti in 2010 that killed close to a quarter million people.

Despite the accolades and fame, he had yet to break a major hip-hop star. His hopes rested on an up-and-coming rapper, The Game, who had a gift for rhyming over just about any style. Sean Combs was interested in signing him to Bad Boy Records, but the rapper got scooped up by Dr. Dre to be part of his newly launched Aftermath Records. The Game would become part of a crew called G-Unit that included 50-Cent, Tony Yayo, and Lloyd Banks. On January 25, 2005, the Game and Henchman went on a Maryland radio station for an interview with DJ Zulu on 93.9 FM. When the DJ made fun of Henchman's Bluetooth earpiece, he and the Game attacked the DJ, which resulted in second-degree assault charges. The charges against the Game got dropped but not the ones against Henchman, who again found himself in court, where Queen Latifa was called up as a character witness.

Rosemond straddled two worlds. He was becoming a mogul in the entertainment industry but couldn't let go of the streets. The success and money weren't enough. No matter how hard he tried to move away from the street life, he couldn't do it. Deep down he was still "Jimmy Ace," and he became involved in another famous hip-hop beef, this time with rapper 50 Cent over the documentary *Infamous Times: The Original 50 Cent.*

Rosemond had made the film as a tribute to his childhood friend Kelvin "50 Cent" Martin, from whom the rapper had taken his name. He wanted the rapper 50 Cent to pay $7,500 for Martin's tombstone, which he wanted to include in the documentary's final shots. Rosemond hounded him for months, but the rapper declined to participate. *How do you take this dude's name and you won't even invest $7,500?* wondered Rosemond. 50 Cent's attorney fired back that none of the DVD's profits had been donated to Martin's family or 50 Cent's G-Unity charity, as promised. Rosemond pulled the Game out of 50 Cent's G-Unit posse. At a concert, the Game shouted "G-G-G-G-U-NOT!" and pantomimed beating a man dressed in a rat costume, which was intended to represent 50 Cent, who was being accused of "dry snitching" in his song "Ghetto Quran."

Jimmy's beef with 50 Cent had attracted the attention of the hip-hop press and along with it even more scrutiny from the feds. Haitian Jack was moved from a state prison to a federal prison, a move some saw as an indication that he would be testifying against Jimmy. In 2005, *Newsweek* reported that Henchman was being investigated for unsolved hip-hop murders, including Tupac's in 1996. The 50 Cent–G-Unit feud reached a boiling point in 2007 when G-Unit member Tony Yayo was accused of slapping Henchman's fourteen-year-old son, who was wearing a Czar Entertainment T-shirt. Yayo was arrested for the incident but received only ten days of community service. It was another G-Unit member, Lowell "Lodi Mack" Fletcher who ultimately took credit for the James Rosemond Jr. assault. Lodi Mack served nine months and was shot and killed two weeks after he was released. Henchman was implicated in the killing.

Following the incident, Henchman wrote an open letter to AllHipHop "This is America! I want to apologize to my family and my support system. Most importantly, to my son; When I asked you to intern as a fourteen-year-old at my office it was because I wanted you to see your father working and have a strong role model. I wanted you to look up to brown and black people in boardrooms rather than in the streets. I was proud of the work I was doing. I never thought when I sent you on that errand, you would be surrounded and assaulted by 50 Cent and four G-Unit grown men with guns for wearing a T-shirt."

It all came crashing down when the feds arrested Henchman, charging him with drug trafficking, money laundering, and witness tampering. Prosecutors alleged Henchman made $11 million annually from his illegal activities. The U.S. Attorney for the Eastern District of New York, described Rosemond as "a thug in a suit." Henchman is now doing multiple life sentences in the feds for drug charges and the murder of G-Unit affiliate Lodi Mack.

"It's hard for me to sit here and justify in my head seven life sentences because someone said I was a drug dealer," said Jimmy Henchman from behind bars in *Unjust Justice*. "All of the money and drugs that they had in the courtroom, none of that belonged to me; they had no tapes, not even a fingerprint of mine. They had nothing. And they made that into where they could take millions of legal money from me—money that I acquired from representing Mike Tyson, the Game, Wyclef, from doing movies. For twenty years I've been in the music business, for y'all to come take my profit, to take my money, to take everything that I've worked for, to take my life is ridiculous. I'm shocked that the justice system works that way."

When Donald Trump lost the election in 2020, there were rumors that he would pardon Rosemond, but the pardon never came and Rosemond remains in prison. Many celebrities and athletes supported Rosemond's pardon, including Akon, Queen Latifah, Wyclef Jean, Mike Tyson, and late actor Michael K. Williams. Infamous Little Haiti street gang Zoe Pound produced *Unjust Justice*, which called for Henchman's release. The support for this former street thug turned music mogul is broad. NFL icon Jim Brown also lobbied Donald Trump on Rosemond's behalf without success. Despite it all Rosemond continues to fight for his freedom. Get knocked down a hundred times, get up a hundred times. Henchman will keep fighting despite the obstacles in front of him.

9

TO COME UP THROUGH THE '80S crack cocaine epidemic in New York City and reinvent yourself as a hustler and not only be relevant but come out on top makes you the ultimate "don." A hustler is someone who knows how to hustle in all arenas, seasons, and levels—whether legal or illegal. To a true hustler, the product may change, but the hustle stays the same. It all reflects the whims of the dollar. *Cash rules everything around me*, as Wu-Tang said.

Kevin Chiles, also known as "KC," was a true hustler. He was born in Asheville, North Carolina, before his mother moved him and his brother to the Bronx and then settled in Harlem. Seeing his mother work hard by constantly putting in overtime to survive and raise two sons in New York City gave Chiles his perspective on life. He learned that being a hustler meant getting results out of tough situations. Chiles learned how to get money at a young age. He packed groceries, shoveled snow, any odd job he could get to help his mom. In high school he started dabbling in the drug trade, selling small quantities of marijuana to other students. It was the beginning of his venture into what they called "the life."

"I saw how good my mom felt about the part I was playing in contributing to the household money with my little hustles," Chiles told *Don Diva Magazine*. "And it made me feel good. I wanted to do more for her. I wanted to take care of her." Chiles was about his business and would make things happen, regardless of the situation. It was this *by any means necessary* attitude that carried him and made him who he was. Chiles was a fast learner and came up in a hustler's paradise—Harlem.

Harlem was a center of African American culture, especially when it came to the arts. The famous Apollo Theater had launched the careers of many Black performers of note, such as Billie Holiday, Stevie Wonder, Sammy Davis Jr., the Jackson Five, and Aretha Franklin. While hip-hop began in the Bronx and spread to other boroughs such as Queens, it was Harlem that culturally set the tone and style, from cars and fashion to the drugs and crime. Many notable gangsters also launched their illegal careers on those same streets, what has become known as the "Black Mecca."

This is where Chiles, who became one of the best to ever do it, sat back and studied everything around him. He had a strong mind for business and loved the challenge of creating moves from nothing and watching them grow. He was competitive, and when it came to money, he had the drive of an ultimate hustler. Chiles was like the Black Grant Cardone of his day.

"It was young guys hustling, posturing for the top spot, motivated as much by taking care of our families as we were by getting girls and having fun," Chiles told *Penthouse*. "The positive economic effects of the era extended well beyond people being able to buy boosted goods at a discount, or purchase TVs and VCRs on the cheap from a crackhead. There were families being fed and clothed. There were people that never had cars or taken a trip finally having the means and opportunity."

Chiles's mother was a branch manager of a bank, and she taught him about taxes, savings bonds, and bank accounts. By the time Chiles was nineteen, he already lived in a condominium, and at twenty-one, he owned his first house in the suburbs of New Jersey. KC was getting a lot of money in Harlem and the Bronx in the late '80s courtesy of the crack cocaine trade. For the young hustlers of the era, it was a quick come up.

This was an era when customers from all walks of life came to buy the drug for a quick high—finance types from Wall Street, lawyers, doctors, middle-class working people, low-income people, street dwellers. All that money coming in added up to thousands, tens of thousands, and sometimes hundreds of thousands daily. Kevin Chiles found himself in the middle of the action. He was present and accounted for. A true hustler on the block.

During his first year in college, KC moved up in the drug game through an uncle who dealt with heroin and cocaine. "I convinced him I was going to do it with or without his help, so he figured it was better that he over-saw what I was doing for safety," KC said in an interview with VladTV. It started with just small quantities of crack cocaine, half-grams and grams, and moved up to regularly picking up to 50 kilos of cocaine weekly from Dominican and Colombian suppliers. He started dealing strictly in Harlem with a crew made up of friends from the Bronx, but the New York City scene was increasingly tough, with cheap crack flooding the streets, which brought intense competition amid ever-shrinking real estate.

"You can potentially squeeze every last dime out of a package break-ing it down to maximize your profit. This still didn't match the money I could make taking my show on the road," said Chiles. And take his show on the road he did—to nearby DC, which was an easy one-hour flight away. Buying airline tickets with cash and no identification, KC and his crew made runs to the capital with ziplock bags of cocaine stuffed in coat pockets, strapped around waists, and stashed up sleeves.

Why grind to direct-sell small quantities to local Harlem crackheads hand-to-hand when mass amounts of product could be sold wholesale to DC crews? Apartments were rented for girlfriends so they could have a place to stay and put in their work. DC in return received Chile and his partners with open arms. The product was good and, most important, it was cheaper than local options. "My cost might have been $20,000 per kilo, allowing me to net $10,000 a kilo, headache-free—no cutting, bagging, etc.," explained Chiles in his autobiography *The Crack Era: The Rise, Fall, and Redemption of Kevin Chiles.*

The up-and-coming hustler was not alone as Harlem claimed many notorious gangsters such as Rich Porter and Alpo who were also on the rise. They all strived to make their presence known and names ring loud in the street, mainly through displays of wealth accumulated in the drug game. "We treated hustling almost like an athletic competition. We all vied for Harlem's top spot," said Chiles in *The Crack Era*. "In early 1987, Azie Faison was at the top of the food chain and feeding many of the young hustlers from Harlem like Rich Porter, Alpo, Jason, Travis, Darryl Barnes, Spencer, T-Money, Twin and a bunch of others. . . . My crew viewed them as the opposition; whether we were even on their radar at the moment or not."

In Harlem it was all about being fly, one-upmanship, and gaining brag-ging rights. Rich Porter and Alpo had convertible BMWs, so Chiles got a custom red Benz shipped from Germany that was a hybrid between a 190 and 300 series with an automatic drop-top. It was a showstopper. As he drove around Harlem to show it off, people rushed to check out his new ride that no one had ever seen before. Unfortunately, flashy cars also drew the wrong kind of attention, and Chiles was often stopped and hassled by police. During one stop, his young cockiness got him locked up and his car impounded. Chiles tried to sell the problem car to DC's drug lord Rayful Edmond, but the deal fell through. Eventually he traded it to some Dominicans for 4 kilos of cocaine just to get it out of his hair.

The young hustler was a regular customer of the street-legend designer Dapper Dan, wearing his custom-made outfits, coats, jackets, and hats and even had some of his car interiors done by the designer. Being that dude who was talked about in Harlem, the Bronx, and all over New York City, KC was known for switching up cars—which were parked at various garages around town—two or three times a day, He paid cash for his vehicles, had them customized at Formula 1 on 57th Street and 11th Avenue, and then routinely flipped them to other hustlers so he could get the next best thing and be the "king of the streets."

"Selling drugs on a major level was essentially a full-time gig," Chiles told *Penthouse*. "To say it was fast-paced probably undersells the drama and events one day could hold. For several years, I was netting around $300K weekly, with the bulk of the money coming from DC, and the rest from New York. I was in my early twenties and you really couldn't tell me anything." To a young hustler who grossed over a million dollars a month, the world was truly his.

Everything depended on your supply and the level you were operating on, however. It might look like an easy job, but in reality, it was dangerous and illegal, and you could lose your freedom or your life. The streets were cutthroat, and as you made plans with your money, others were too. It was a game of *get or get got*. The stakes were high and the cost could be higher. KC was determined to be the one to get it all. He saw the pitfalls of the life and did everything he could to avoid them.

"The money was intoxicating," Chiles wrote in his autobiography. "And while it came with a price, none of us were going to turn it down. Once the violence started becoming a regular thing, me and my crew began not only carrying weapons at all times, but wearing bulletproof vests and sometimes even bulletproof hats as well. Instead of changing our mindset and environment, we just adapted to the madness." Evolve or die was the mindset. No one was willing to walk away from the game, not with all the money involved. Hustlers just tried to stay one step ahead of the competition and the gun thugs plotting to rip them off.

The game in Harlem attracted a lot of attention, from women to admirers to people who wanted to get in with you and your team to stickup kids and kidnappers to police trying to bust you. When cats started getting money, cars, and jewelry there were others lying in wait to take it. Groups like Clarence Heatley's "Preacher Crew," the "Young Guns," and the "Lynch Mob" had earned a reputation not just for drug dealing, but robbing, killing, and extorting.

Some white guys even got into the robbing and kidnapping by wearing fake badges and pretending to be cops. The various stickup crews often turned against one another and an arms race ensued. Hustlers who had once collected cars and sneakers were now buying weapons *en masse*. Chiles reflected that "our stash houses were stockpiled with so many weapons and body armor you might have thought we were a private militia training to overthrow a Central American nation." It paid to be armed to the teeth rather than get caught slipping.

"It created anarchy, renegades, and increased drama. Violence, kidnapping, and murders," Chiles told *Penthouse*. "There were no rules, and the younger generation and up-and-coming hustlers didn't really fear the repercussions. It was like *Lord of the Flies* on steroids. Having the most guns, and the biggest guns, along with a big crew, was deemed to serve as a form of deterrence."

KC knew he had to step up his game to survive, not only in the streets, but where he stayed, so he could remain free and alive to enjoy the fruits of his illicit gains. Being a business-minded man with a mother who knew business, banking, and accounting, KC started transitioning out of the game and opening legal businesses. He was forward-thinking and knew that a long run in the streets wasn't in the cards. Plus, the violence was getting out of hand. He decided to get out while he could. Before he was swallowed whole and eaten alive.

It was a standard practice for the Harlem hustlers to sink their illegitimate earnings into establishing legitimate business fronts. Drug lords and kingpins opened up bars, restaurants, barber shops, and grocery stores. KC and his crew were already spending thousands to fill their closets with the freshest gear and the newest, limited-edition sneakers. At the time, the number-one place for anyone with wealth to outfit themselves was at A. J. Lester. It seemed only natural for KC to open up his own sneaker shop, and he chose a location right across the street from the famous A. J.'s. It was both a case of positioning himself where everyone with means was already shopping, but also part of his competitive nature and a way to further establish himself as "boss."

BOSS Sneakers opened in 1998 on 8th Avenue between 125th and 126th Streets in the heart of Harlem's retail district. "Sneaker culture was as big then as it is now. You would go to our houses and we had two hundred to three hundred pairs of sneakers in our closet," said Chiles in an interview with VladTV. "For me, I said to myself 'I have thirty friends and we all making money. If I didn't sell nothing to anybody but them I would have a successful business.'"

KC claims that he made $15,000 on opening day, mainly from sales to his own crew. The store became a place for him to hold court when he wasn't traveling to DC running drugs and stacking dollars. But the business game didn't stop with BOSS Sneakers. KC's next venture was BOSS Emporium, a fashion store that brought big-name designer fashion to Harlem. The Emporium was KC's ode to street culture and featured TVs tuned to *Yo! MTV Raps*, murals of Rucker Park, and a tricked-out BMW 3 Series in the front window. BOSS Emporium was the talk of Harlem.

Hustlers flocked to the store as did all the neighborhood people. As soon as word spread about the Emporium, big-time names like Mike Tyson, LL Cool J, Teddy Riley, and even Tupac showed up. The store was buzzing all over the city, and drug dealers and hustlers from every borough stopped by, just wanting to purchase something from the trendy store. People would go to BOSS just to be seen there. The business ventures did more than outfit Harlem and create a buzz, they also helped Chiles launder the millions of dollars he was bringing in. He was turning the illicit into a legit avenue.

The money also helped KC support his first love growing up—street basketball. And in Harlem nothing was bigger than the Rucker, or "Entertainers Basketball Classic." These summer street-ball tournaments became the place in Harlem to see and be seen. But tournament founder Greg Marius was having trouble making it profitable and money ran short. So Marius enlisted Chiles to bridge the gap and close the season. "I gave Greg the money to pay for trophies, referees fees, and anything else needed so he was able to maintain the tournament," said Chiles.

KC even got together his own Rucker team called the BOSS All Stars, which cost several thousand dollars per game for cab money, expensive team dinners, and cash gifts to his elite players. Because of Chiles's avid support of street ball, Puff Daddy approached him to throw a celebrity basketball game with the rapper Heavy D. Thousands showed up at the City College gym in Manhattan, which created a stampede that killed nine people, a tragic event that marred the intent and got tons of bad publicity.

KC was involved with other business ventures: He had holdings in a restaurant on 129th and Lenox in Harlem, two laundromats, Take No Shorts management, and BOSS Records (made through a connection with Bernard Thomas, who had worked with Eric B. and Rakim for Robert Hill's Zakia Records). It is alleged that Zakia Records was also started with money from the streets. Chiles had producers who made it later but were with KC before they blew up, such as Dame Grease. BOSS Records showcased their portfolio of artists at the 1994 Jack the Rapper music convention, at which KC was offered several major-label distribution deals. KC was also in negotiations with clothes designer Karl Kani to manufacture his own clothing line. It seemed to be all coming together for him.

As KC was riding high, tragedy struck. Opportunistic stickup kids had kidnapped his partner's girlfriend, Sarray Watson, in an attempt to extort money. Watson took them to Chile's mother's house where they made their demands. Barbara Chiles, a bank manager with no criminal ties, had little to offer and things went from bad to worse. "My mother, Barbara Chiles, along with two other women, Rita Faulk and Sarray Watson, were all tied and bound, before being shot in the head. Sarray was the only survivor," Chiles told *Penthouse*. "My mother was killed by cowards. If they wanted me, I wasn't hard to find. I was usually at my store, BOSS Sneakers, on 125th Street in Harlem. My mother's murder was another loud declaration that we were dealing with a different kind of savage in the crack era, who followed no rules or code of ethics."

Despite the tragedy, KC balled out of control but switched lanes and got all-the-way legit. He stayed that brand-name dude in Harlem. He remained strong and focused, grinding hard on his record-label hustle, and was determined to leave the game behind and focus on his legitimate business ventures. But the feds had other plans—they were already investigating the Harlem hustler and burgeoning businessman.

Around 1992, KC noticed that he was being tailed by a car with tinted windows. He didn't know if it was the law or another stickup kid looking to make a score. He'd had a good long run and had watched several of his contemporaries get killed or put behind bars. In 1990, Rich Porter was found dead in the Bronx a month after his nephew had been mutilated and killed in a kidnapping. In 1991, Alpo was sentenced to thirty-five years for various drug charges and the killing of DC drug lord Michael "Fray" Salters. Chiles had lived with the fear that he might end up dead, but the idea of being surveilled by the law enforcement was a novelty.

Through an FBI connection, he was told he was being watched, which had been confirmed by a business associate the feds had questioned. Of the Harlem hustlers, he was the last man standing, and it seemed his time was coming. KC became paranoid and began folding up his drug enterprise, selling off DC apartments, using burner phones, buying call scramblers, and sweeping his office for bugs. But his efforts to lay low failed and he was arrested in 1994. The feds were determined to make an example of the rap impresario.

"Over the course of a two-year investigation and more than 8,500 taped conversations, my arrest did not include one piece of evidence that suggested I was selling drugs," Chiles told *Penthouse*. "However, the charges against so many of my family members and acquaintances showed me the government's strategy. They were trying to force a plea or cooperation from me with the threat of incarcerating my loved ones, despite the fact that they never had any role in the drug game other than benefiting from my generosity."

Chiles had two mistrials before he entered a plea and got sentenced to ten years in prison. Unlike most name-brand dudes whose stories end when they come to prison, KC found a way to become even bigger, to the point where his name is known not only everywhere in the United States but worldwide. While in prison KC formed a team who created an avenue that would help people tell their stories and share them with the world. It was a magazine, but this one was like no other. It became known as the "Outlaw's Bible."

The renowned *Don Diva Magazine* happened by accident. Chile's girlfriend Tiffany wanted to break into the music industry by managing a stripper turned rapper named Bonnie Clyde. A buzz needed to be created, and KC thought they should create a promotional picture book. He collected some photographs of old-school hustlers and street legends who were being name-dropped by the hip-hop artists who came from the streets. The promotional "yearbook" included ads for Bonnie Clyde. Although the book was intended to be a free promotional item, people began reselling copies for twenty dollars.

In his autobiography, Chiles explained that "we had no idea we had just printed the premier issue of what would be known as *Don Diva Magazine: The Original Street Bible*. Soon after the booklet hit the streets, Tiff started getting letters asking when the next issue was coming out and how could they get a subscription?" The magazine was a hit in prison, on the streets, and in the hip-hop world.

This magazine became so successful that copycat magazines followed what Kevin Chiles created. So, KC being KC, he raised the bar even higher. *Don Diva* started featuring legal cases and became a helpful resource for men and women in prison. He also started providing a pen-pal service and added pages that featured models. *Don Diva* even began hosting parties and events in cities across the country. The magazine became a lifestyle brand and started getting large sponsorship checks from Def Jam Records and others.

According to Cavario H., a journalist who worked on the magazine in the early days, "Don" represented a man who was at the top of his game, and "Diva" was a woman who was at the top of her game. *Don Diva* fit KC to a T, even though his name never appeared on the masthead. All of his life he had competed to become the "don" of Harlem. Along the way he stood tall and continued standing tall. The "Original Street Bible" paid tribute to the game he had played—as a hustler, drug dealer, businessman, entertainment executive, and ultimately incarcerated prisoner. Like BOSS Emporium before it, *Don Diva* showcased a man's love for the street and kept it real—as real as Kevin Chiles, the Harlem hustler himself.

THE TALE OF PUFF DADDY'S BODYGUARD

MAN

Bad Boy Records and Anthony "Wolf"

10

SEAN "PUFF DADDY" COMBS IS A HIP-HOP CELEBRITY. From A&R man at Uptown to riding shotgun with Biggie Smalls at Bad Boy to the East Coast–West Coast beef, Combs has always been front and center. A pretty boy from Harlem who could dance, produce, spot talent, promote, and rap, he was a born star. But dudes who know the score have always said Combs is the type of dude who had a real gangster on his team.

"P. Diddy had real thugs and killers in his circle," said "A-Man," who is doing two life sentences in the feds at USP McCreary. The Newport News, Virginia, native was running drugs and doing big things down in the VA in the late '80s until he got arrested and convicted in the late '90s on drug-conspiracy charges. All the hustlers who plied their trade in any of the cities in the eastern part of Virginia knew who the fuck A-Man was.

"Puff had this one cat on his team who was running around in New York and bounced to Virginia Beach, Virginia, back in the late '80s, early '90s," A-Man said. "His name was Anthony Jones, but heads knew him as 'Wolf.' Dude was definitely about his business and that gunplay. He wasn't nothing to fuck with."

A-Man continued: "Eastwood, Hitler, and Charlie Dog from the BX was out there and them cats Kelly Blue and his crew from Queens was all out there. That's the team Al Monday and Shakim Bio was eating with. Teddy Riley, Q-Tip, all those New York cats was out there. Wolf was out there too on some enforcer shit for the Butt Naked Entertainment squad. They were eating lovely."

When Puff got fired from Uptown Records, he was fucking with Butt Naked. They were promoting parties in Virginia. Wolf was with them. And when a Butt Entertainment member named El and others got indicted, Wolf got indicted too. He went to trial and got acquitted. Wolf was always lucky like that. A gunslinging rude boy who kept it gully. It wasn't about fronting; it was about putting in that work, and Wolf was down for the gunplay.

"Wolf was a Johnny Romance handsome thug cat, who kept all the fly chicks on his dick, but he bussed those guns and was known as Gunsmoke Wolf," Shakim Bio said. "He wasn't scared to let those bullets loose. When he got acquitted in the '90s on that federal case in Virginia, he got with Puff, who was popping with Bad Boy Entertainment and got on some bodyguard shit. He was Puffy's street guy."

Born on February 20, 1965, Anthony "Wolf" Jones, who allegedly got his nickname for styling his hair like Eddie Munster from *The Munsters* TV show—with a werewolf's widow's peak and sideburns—was an original gangsta who kept it real at all times. After hooking up with Puffy, he became that dude who made guys think twice about fucking with the ambitious and outgoing music mogul. With Wolf on his team, Puffy could do what the fuck he wanted without recourse or retaliation.

"A lot of cats don't like Puffy, but they are too timid to cross Wolf, who is like Puffy's extra arm," an anonymous hip-hop impresario told the *Village Voice* in a 2001 piece titled "Big Bad Wolf." "He was part guardian angel, part wolf." Putting himself in the way of any drama that came at Puffy, he was the wall that stopped the hate, the innuendos, and the violence. The media and law enforcement tried to portray Wolf as a reckless ex-con and gun thug, but those in the know considered him a cunning adversary and true gangsta who followed the G code and saved people just because he felt like it. An avenging angel who used violence as an equalizer.

"If there's any creature like that, Wolf definitely is the one," an Atlanta-based bodyguard told the *Village Voice*. "Once I was about to be locked up and the guardian angel part of him stepped in when no one else would." Loyalty was important to Wolf, as was looking out for his people and those who looked out for him. That is why Puffy had him by his side at all times. He knew what type of dude Wolf was and the lengths he would be willing to go if trouble arose. Some dudes talk that gangsta shit, but when a real gangsta walks into the room, people know.

"Wolf looks out for a lot of people," the president of a rival security agency told the *Village Voice*. "He put my guys on to a lot of work, got us in the game. He was not intimidated by us. He would sit down at the table and we would argue back and forth with him." Wolf was smart and knew having allies was important. You never knew when you might need some assistance. And a posse of guys with guns that know how to use them is never a bad thing.

On September 23, 1995, at the Platinum City club in Atlanta, there was a big birthday party for superstar producer and "So So Def" label-owner Jermaine Dupri. All the big music executives were out there. Puff was there showing out with his team. And Wolf was there watching his back. Wasn't no faking it. The Wolf always had Puffy's back.

Suge Knight was also there with his Death Row Records cats. Puff and Suge had differences, but it wasn't serious. Competition existed between them—some arrogance about who was going to come out on top—but this was way before the East Coast–West Coast rap beef that claimed Tupac and Biggie's lives. But Suge was versed in violence and Puff wouldn't let anything go. He played the diplomat, but deep down Puff was gangsta too.

"Both [Puffy and Suge] entered the game at the same time as label owners and both wanted to be the next big thing," Shakim Bio said. "Next thing you know it went to words and then guns were drawn and shots were fired. Knight's bodyguard Jake 'Big Jake' Robles, a twenty-four-year-old Compton gang member, who was an executive with Death Row Records, was shot and killed in front of the club. Word was that was Wolf's work."

But no one was talking and Wolf didn't brag about it, so cops had nothing to go on. That didn't mean he wasn't the main suspect. "It was gossiped in Atlanta that Wolf did it," a friend of Jones told the *Village Voice*. "Most of the cops assumed that he was the one who did the killing, but they had their doubts, plus if there was a major problem at their spots, Wolf was the only one, for some reason, who could arbitrate a peaceful outcome."

It was reported that Jones, who was thirty-seven days away from completing a parole term for a 1991 attempted-murder conviction, wasn't looking for trouble that night. "Wolf went there as advance man for the Bad Boy camp, making sure everything was straight, setting up how Puff's gonna come in, when he gonna come in," Jones's friend told the *Village Voice*.

Suge was already at the club, flanked by Big Jake, the three-hundred-pound ex-con gangbanger, and a bunch of OG Crips from Cali. "They started banging on Wolf, saying stuff like, 'You and that buster you're with, nigga, what up?'" Jones's friend continued, "Wolf and them didn't sweat it, they wasn't worried because they felt it wasn't a big deal. Rivalries like this come up all the time."

But when Big Jake starting mouthing off, Wolf just laid back and didn't say anything. He just crossed his arms. "And when certain people don't talk, that's when it's time to shut up because shit happens," said the friend. "Now it's Wolf and Suge, eye to eye, waiting for the next move. Then shots rang out, and that's when everybody jump in cars and jet off." Suge never let that shit go. The beef was personal before it got lyrical with their artists. Wolf seemed to always be in the middle of some drama when it came to Puff. But then again that's what he was paid to do.

"Wolf was there when Puff smacked up Steve Stoute with a champagne bottle in Stoute's office," Shakim Bio said. "But don't be fooled, he just fingered Puff. Wolf probably the one who roughed Steve up like that. Ain't no one telling on Wolf. So he fingered Puff knowing Puff going pay his way out that shit. Puff is paid and fly, you know."

Shakim Bio added: "When Scar threw that mitt of money in Puff's face in Club New York back in 1999—Puff was with his then-girlfriend Jennifer Lopez—he had his artist Shine with him and Wolf. Wolf wasn't having that shit. He let loose in that piece, shot that spot all up. A chick got shot in the face too. Shine got popped with a gun; they knocked Wolf and Puff."

It was a highly publicized case, and Jennifer Lopez had no idea what she had gotten into with Puff Daddy as her boyfriend. They ran from the police and tried to bribe the driver to take the gun. They went to trial on that case and Puffy hired Johnnie Cochran. Wolf and Puffy got acquitted, but Shine took the rap and got ten years in the state. It seemed like Wolf was beating cases like the "Dapper Don" and it just made him more reckless in the streets. He started thinking he was untouchable.

"Wolf was known to air shit out," A-Man said. "And he kept all the fly bitches too. Pretty-boy thug Wolf. Bitches loved him. Dudes loved to be in his company. You were safe with Wolf having your back. He was that nigga for real, but his downfall was those females. He had so many and felt that he owned them." When dudes start tripping over females and get in their feelings, that's a bad look. It's supposed to be like Jay-Z rapped, *I got 99 problems but a bitch ain't one.*

It's often said in the streets that *when you live by the gun you die by the gun,* and that would happen with Wolf. He was back down in the ATL in November 2003, at another Jermaine Dupree party in fact, when he got into it in a club. Wolf was arguing with one of the women that he used to fuck with. She was hanging hard with the BMF crew, Big Meech and them, and Wolf didn't like it. He was that dude and didn't like that the up-and-coming Big Meech was stealing his shine.

"He felt some kind of way," A-Man said. "Like she was disrespecting him by being out in the presence of something else. On his level, or should I say way bigger in stature than Wolf was at the time. So it could have been a number of things. Wolf roughed shorty up, pulling on her, and security got involved and told Wolf to chill out and when he barked on them Big Meech stepped in and said something and it was on."

A-Man added: "Neither gangsta would back down. It was the Big Bad Wolf and Big Meech show. The club was silent. Watching as the drama unfolded. But security was all on Meech's dick. He was the one throwing money around. So they grabbed Wolf and escorted him out of the club. Problem solved. Or so they thought." But when you cross a gangsta in public it's never over. Wolf had to do something or his reputation would be in tatters.

Wolf was livid and felt supremely disrespected. He knew he had to save face or things would never be the same for him. There was no way he was getting embarrassed by Big Meech. Wolf went and got his guy Lamont "Riz" Girdy, who was a known shooter and, Wolf being Wolf, they posted up on Big Meech's car until Meech and his entourage came out of the club. It was on and popping.

After that shots were fired from all sides. Big Meech ran and caught a hot one in the buttocks, but when the shots stopped and the smoke cleared, there were two bodies lying dead in the parking lot—Anthony "Wolf" Jones and Lamont "Riz" Girdy. The Wolf's reign in the streets was over. Puffy's bodyguard was dead. Street justice had been dispensed and Wolf was caught wanting.

PART 3

2000s
Gangsta Rap
Rules

HIP-HOP GANGSTA CHRONICLES IN THE 305

MIA

Rick Ross, Boobie Boys, and Slip-N-Slide Records

11

WHEN PEOPLE TALK OF CRIME AND GANGSTERS in Miami, what often gets lost are the stories of its hood stars. We've all heard of the "Cocaine Cowboys" and Griselda Blanco, aka the "Black Widow," but what about those who plied their trade in the ghetto with no fanfare?

The hood side of Miami is known for a lot of things—"donk" cars, Miami bass, "choppa" fire throughout the night, homegrown street legends like Bunky Brown and Rick Brownlee, and sections like Liberty City, which has been one of Miami's most notorious hoods since the '80s and took a start turn in Grand Theft Auto.

In 1937, the federal government built the Liberty Square Houses for Black families who outgrew nearby Overtown. "The white families in Liberty City were so panicked about all these poor blacks moving in that the city actually built a wall that ran down the middle of Twelfth Avenue, from Sixty-Second Street to Seventy-First Street, to separate the new projects from the white part of town," said 2 Live Crew's Luther "Luke" Campbell, a resident of Liberty City, in his autobiography, *The Book of Luke*. "By the time I was a kid, [the projects] was already falling apart. There was no investment from the city to keep them nice. Eventually nobody called it Liberty Square anymore. Everyone called it Pork 'n' Beans, because that's all the people that lived there could afford to eat."

When the Civil Rights Act of 1964 coincided with the building of Interstate 95, a number of lower-income and welfare-dependent families migrated from Overtown to Liberty City, which altered the neighborhood dramatically. By the late '70s, Liberty City was poor in every way, but when the crack cocaine epidemic hit in the '80s, it made a bad situation worse. Liberty City had second-rate housing and schools. Kids growing up there wanted to do better, but role models were scarce and they just followed the path set before them. It was a vicious cycle of poverty that the homegrown gangsters would exploit.

One of the famous hood stars from Liberty City was Richard Simmons, who was known in the area as "Convertible Burt" because of his taste in automobiles. Burt was getting tons of money from the cocaine trade in the mid-'80s. Every car he had was either foreign or a convertible, and his collection included a stretch limousine, an Oldsmobile Delta 88, a Cadillac, and a Rolls-Royce. He even had some of the cars customized at chop-shops, directing them to cut off the tops. Rolling through the hood in luxury, he was a local celebrity and lightning rod. Showing the young boys what life could bring. "That donk [Miami custom-car] culture came from me," said Burt an interview with VladTV. "That's what I created."

"I grew up on 15th Avenue, which was one of the main drug strips in the country at the time in the '80s," said Burt. "When I started getting into [the drug trade] it was like everything was environmental, you know what I'm saying. I didn't choose the game, the game chose me—coming up and being in that environment and just being exposed to so much at a very young age." Burt got his start in elementary school, where his extra-curricular activities included being a lookout for the older drug dealers in the street. It was a criminal education that would pay off handsomely for the ten-year-old.

In the late '80s with the crack cocaine epidemic raging nationwide, there was such a surplus of dealers and suppliers that risk outweighed reward. Prices plummeted as suppliers undercut their competitors to get rid of excess inventory. The demand for the product was consistent, but profit margins were not. As Miami became ground zero for cocaine imports from South America, the city was covered with snow valued in the billions of dollars. Finding a connect was easy and business was cutthroat. The Colombians killed off their competitors without hesitation.

Suppliers started to look outside of Florida to places where the product wasn't readily available. Convertible Burt became one of Miami's first hood stars to move cocaine up I-95 and out into the rest of the country. First stop: Atlanta, Georgia. "The Miami boys originally started with me and a couple of guys who started going on the road," Convertible Burt told VladTV. "We started going to different parts of the United States getting money and that's how we started founding the Miami Boys. We got a different swag in Miami so whenever we'd go somewhere they be so much with us, they pretty much gave us the name the 'Miami Boys.'"

At the time Atlanta was just becoming the new Black Mecca. Burt flooded the ghetto and suburban areas with cocaine and made a huge profit, much more than he did back in Miami. With his wild Miami swag, Burt became a celebrity in Atlanta and hung out with players from the Hawks and Falcons. He also got back to Miami and socialized with Dolphins and Heat players and even hobnobbed there with Mike Tyson. "Back then, I was young. I brought the world heavyweight champion Mike Tyson down here," Burt said. "I was doing big things. I was getting so much money."

Convertible Burt became the guy who everybody wanted to take a ride with. He was their hood pass to enter Liberty City's danger zones as they partied and jammed to the Miami bass music being popularized by Luther Campbell, aka "Luke Skyywalker," and the 2 Live Crew. As Burt drove through the hood, he would blast their songs through his badass, top-of-the-line stereo. The earthquake bass rumbled from blocks away to announce his presence. "A lot of this rap culture, you know what I'm saying, they wasn't even rapping about convertibles until I put that into play," Burt said.

Since its birth much of hip-hop's basic formula remains the same, but new elements have always been added to it. One of the things Miami brought was the heavy bass sound, and the man who brought it to the mainstream was Liberty City's own Luke Skyywalker (later "Uncle Luke") with his 2 Live Crew as well as the acts MC Shy D and JT Money/Poison Clan. It was Luke who created a blueprint that not only helped him become rich and successful but others as well. "I take my hat off to people like Luther Campbell. I seen Luke [start an independent label]. He opened doors for us in South Florida," said Ted Lucas of Slip-N-Slide Records, which has featured artists such as Trick Daddy and Rick Ross.

"Luke Records started with nothing, came from nothing, just a twenty-five-year-old DJ a few months out of cooking in a hospital kitchen, out hustling gigs in one of the most fucked-up, riot-torn ghettos in America," Campbell said in his autobiography, *The Book of Luke*. "I always had to do everything on my own since I was an outsider. . . . Being in Miami, I was considered a nobody, an outcast by the music industry. There was no road map for a rapper to build his own record company. Nobody in New York was doing it. Nobody in LA was doing it."

At first Luke's DJ crew purchased gear by hustling weed and providing party music. But once the 2 Live Crew took off, Luke Records sold 750,000 records in its first year. And though he was now legitimate, he had problems with law enforcement and politicians for what they considered obscene raps. "We had sheriffs coming after us, city councils coming after us. We had judges, lawyers, the PTA," Luke said. "We even had Vice President Dan Quayle making statements about us."

He embraced the image. "If I'm the bad guy, I'll be the bad guy; if that's the role they want me to play, I'll play it to the hilt," Luke said. "If white folks were scared of the big, bad, oversexed Black man, I'd be the biggest, baddest, nastiest, dirtiest, oversexed Black man they could possibly imagine—just to prove that I could be. Just to prove that I had the right to be if I wanted." This attitude birthed his biggest album, *As Nasty as They Wanna Be*. With explicit songs like "Pop That Pussy" and "Me So Horny," record stores got busted for carrying the record and Campbell was forced to the front lines to successfully defend his right to free speech. A big reason artists today are allowed to say what they want on their records is because of those efforts on the part of Uncle Luke.

Convertible Burt was one of the hood stars who hung out with Uncle Luke. Luke got that ultimate street cred and Burt got to be famous— instead of infamous—because anyone in the underworld knows there's a difference. Luke would have his stable of all-star dancers grinding up on Burt who flossed with his jewelry, convertibles, and endless cash flow. With so much money in play, Burt made legitimate business moves buying up property and stores. He started a record company with Beatmaster Clay D and Rahiem right around the time the Get Funky Crew released an underground single called "Shake Them Titties." The song name drops Burt in the intro and is a big bass boomer shouting out love for everything Miami, from convertibles to bikinis to breasts. But Burt's transition to the music industry was short lived, as the feds had other plans for the hustler.

Convertible Burt set the template for the Miami D-Boy and hustlers who came later. As one drug kingpin emerged, another ended up getting killed or jailed for life. For Richard "Convertible Burt" Simmons, it was the latter. He got arrested by the DEA in 1992 and sentenced to almost thirty years in federal prison. In the Convertible Burt era, there weren't too many big drug dealers, but by the early 1990s there were hundreds if not thousands of kingpins coming out of Miami's projects like Burt. When he went down, others wised up and figured out another way to come up in the hood. A few were smart enough to find a legal hustle. Ted Lucas was one of them.

Growing up in Liberty City, being poor was something that felt natural until you saw what was on the other side of the bridge on Collins Avenue. Before that the only role models you had were athletes, entertainers, or hood stars who came from the same neighborhood. While the wealthy jet-set class made Miami Beach a prime destination and shopped on Ocean Drive, options in the hood were limited. The drug lords who had been street superstars in Miami were locked away or six feet under. It was just the nature of the beast.

Ted Lucas was determined to make it in life. He saw what the culture of hip-hop had created in his community and he felt how it had impacted him. He saw the music industry as a surefire moneymaker. Record companies were generating way too much money for him to be left out. Ted started out as a club promoter—booking acts, bringing them to Miami—but that quickly progressed.

"When I first started, Miami was known for booty-shakin' and bass music," Lucas told *HipHopDX* in 2014. "I loved that type of music, I felt like I wanted to represent my city [differently than] the booty-shaking. There's two sides, there's the other side of the bridge, on South Beach. I wanted to show Miami from my point of view, the way I grew up. This is the way a lot of the kids from the hood see it. That's what I was trying to capture and put in the spotlight from when I first started."

Promoting parties in the Miami hip-hop scene connected Lucas to Miami hustlers. Always looking to connect with people making moves, Lucas started meeting the guys who spent big money for VIP treatment, expensive champagne, and buying out the bar just to show they can. Cats just being known for being *the one to know* for whatever you might need. Kenneth "Boobie" Williams was one of those dudes. Known as "Black" to some, but "Boobie" to others, Williams was a mover and shaker in Miami's gangster underworld. A certified gangsta who demanded respect.

Boobie came from Carol City, but he was known throughout Miami City. His headquarters was at the "Matchbox" projects in Opa-Locka. In

1987 he sold small quantities of cocaine before he moved on to robbing and shooting other drug dealers. He drove around in stolen cars armed with high-powered assault rifles. His uniform was a ski mask and head-to-toe camouflage as he robbed large quantities of drugs that he resold. After being locked up as a suspect in numerous murders and robberies, he pled guilty to attempted murder and got sentenced to prison time.

While he was incarcerated, Boobie created a blueprint for a drug trafficking operation that, when implemented upon his release, would make him a Miami hood star. As head of that operation, he allegedly supervised the supply and distribution of cocaine to a network of drug wholesalers who supplied the drugs to other brokers including small-time dealers who sold it in the streets of Miami and elsewhere. Boobie was a modern-day Frank White. Everything went through him.

The Feds labeled the distribution crew the "Boobie Boys." The Boobie Boys were not a stereotypical "gang" with colors, hand signals, or other visible signs of membership, but rather an informal association of people from the Miami area who were all connected to the man known as Boobie. It was alleged that Boobie had a Panamanian connect and was getting 300 to 500 kilos of pure cocaine at a time.

"The name Boobie Boys was something that the media came up with to identify the case," Arthur "Plex" Pless told *Don Diva Magazine*. "Boobie was who the crackers really wanted, so that's what they labeled their files. Black was the homie, niggas respected him because he was one hundred percent real, but he ain't have no boys and we weren't no gang."

The Boobie Boys story became much bigger than the Convertible Burt stories, however, in part because of the rise to fame of William Roberts and Ted Lucas. Boobie's crew allegedly ran the Carol City, Overtown, Opa-Locka, and Liberty City sections of Miami and had several wars with other drug gangs such as the Thomas Brothers and Avonda Dowling's crew, known as "Vonda's Gang." The feds said that the Boobie Boys were responsible for over seventeen murders in the city of Miami and had a network of distributors in other places such as Georgia and Virginia.

"Boobie was different," wrote Rick Ross in his autobiography, *Hurricanes*. "He didn't drink, smoke, or even use profane language. His leadership was rooted in finesse. He was a person who people genuinely liked and wanted to be associated with. Now don't get it fucked up, Boobie was by far the most on-go nigga in the history of Carol City. He did not hesitate to drop the hammer when a situation called for it and he felt like the situation called for it a lot."

In 1994 Ted Lucas formed Slip-N-Slide Records after he decided that his dreams for making it to the NFL weren't going to happen. "I was one of those kids in the inner city who knew they were going to make it to the NFL for football. Then I get to college and realize everybody ain't going to the NFL. So I'm sitting in my college dorm room and just said, 'What do you like to do?' You got to find your passion. . . . Music was it," Lucas said in an interview with the podcast *Trapital*.

He couldn't rap. He couldn't sing. But Lucas had a gift for recognizing talent, and after he finished college, he got to work. He found a few artists to work with and formed the record label. He admitted that his original batch of artists weren't very good, but he found a gem in an incarcerated rapper known as "Trick Daddy Dollars" who was spoken highly of by the rapper's brother, Hollywood.

Lucas helped fund Trick Daddy's defense to get him home from prison. He sat him down and said, "If you can stay out of trouble, I would take every dollar I got and fulfill what your brother [Hollywood] seen in you." Trick Daddy Dollars debuted in 1997 with his local album *Based on a True Story*, but the distributor was lukewarm. The album didn't fit the mold that Luke had established for South Florida booty-shaking music. But when the preorders came in, they knew it would be a hit.

Trick would break into the mainstream with his next release, www.thug.com, after dropping "Dollars" from his moniker. Trick Daddy's second album included the hit single "Nann Nigga," which featured a new female rapper, Trina, who was also from Liberty City and signed to Slip-N-Slide Records. As owner of an independent label, it was a weekly grind for Lucas, as he had to hand-deliver their records to shops all over Florida and to flea-market vendors. But the hard work paid off and he ended up selling millions of records.

Slip-N-Slide is affiliated closely with Miami-based Poe Boy Music Group (formerly Poe Boy Entertainment), which was founded by Ted Lucas's close friend Elric "E Class" Prince and his brother, Elvin "Big Chuck" Prince. Ted Lucas and E-Class, who are both from Liberty City, were associated with Kenneth "Boobie" Williams before any of them blew up. Slip-N-Slide went on to sign acts like F$O Dinero, Mike Smiff, Plies, Swazy, Pitbull Shonie, J Shin, Sebastian Mikael, Mya Phillmore,

Teenear, and singing group Jagged Edge. On the other hand, Poe Boy Music Group, which was founded in 1999, signed rappers Cognito, UK DJ/producer Gav Savar, J Rand, Kulture Shock, Yung Max, Jacki-O, Young GQ, Brisco, and Flo Rida.

Lucas struck gold again when he signed rapper William Roberts. Roberts came from the Carol City section of Miami and was a big husky kid since middle school who stood out playing football through junior high and high school and seemed destined for the NFL. At the same time Roberts was highly influenced by hip-hop culture and mesmerized by rap music, as he grew up listening to the greats of the late '80s and early '90s such as Run-DMC, LL Cool J, Big Daddy Kane, the Geto Boys, Ice T, N.W.A., and of course Miami's own 2 Live Crew.

Hip-hop was a big part of his life—as much as football. When William got injured playing football, he knew that his athletic career was over and he would never play professionally. But he had another talent that would make him famous. William Roberts could rap.

Roberts would become known as "Rick Ross," taking his name from the West Coast cocaine kingpin "Freeway" Ricky Ross. In the video for his breakout single "Hustlin'" he includes a spoken-word intro about his home: *Miami the playboy's paradise. Pretty girls. Fast cars. That's just a facade. The bridge separates South Beach from my Miami—the real Miami. With the M-I-Yayo. This is where we hustle."* When DJ Khaled premiered the song on 99 Jamz he stretched the four-minute track into an hour-long banger. Other area DJs followed, playing the song so much they got in trouble with program managers and club promoters. All of Miami was behind Rick Ross.

Ross released two albums under the Slip-N-Slide label, 2006's *Port of Miami* and 2008's *Trilla*. With Ted Lucas's blessing, Ross left and started a music publishing company for the songs he wrote. Ross's rap style was "Cocaine Kingpin" rap, in which he told vivid stories about selling tons of cocaine throughout Miami and beyond and having ties to the "Real Noriega" who owed him "favors." And of course he name-dropped the godfather of Miami, rhyming, *I touch work like Convertible Burt.*

To establish his street cred, Ross connected himself to the Boobie Boys story. It wasn't unusual for rappers to name-drop street legends, but Ross took it to another level. On every album he recorded, at least one song refers to his affiliation with the Boobie Boys. In "Hustlin'" Ross rhymed

When they snatched Black, I cried for a hundred nights. Ross even wore T-shirts that had "Boobie Boys" spelled out on the front.

On his 2014 album *Hood Billionaire*, Ross got Boobie to call in from the federal Bureau of Prisons and recorded his calls to use as interludes between songs. "Boobie and I had stayed in touch ever since he got locked up but this was the first time he allowed me to feature him in my music," wrote Ross in his autobiography. To get Boobie's voice on the album as he was doing multiple life sentences solidified Ross reputation in the streets, even though he was simply piggybacking on the relationships that Ted Lucas and E-Class had already established.

Ross is a brilliant storyteller and a standout wordsmith, but his ties to the Boobie Boys may not be exactly as he claims. It's well known that his street credibility came into question when photos leaked of him working as a correctional officer as a young man. Either way, Ross's authenticity will be questioned forever because in the end rap music is just art, and the real ones who were involved in the streets know *the real from the fake.* One way or another, there is always a connection, a link, an instance in which someone knows someone and the truth gets out.

Ross's many incidents—such as the confrontation with Detroit's Trick-Trick, or even the Gangster Disciples for throwing Larry Hoover's name in the "BMF" (Blowing Money Fast) song or being shot at, threatened, and allegedly extorted—speak to his reputation in the streets, not the rap world. Many think it was Kenneth "Boobie" Williams who was using his influence to get Ross out of these situations.

In the end, Miami provided the template for big bass party music through independent entrepreneurs like Luther Campbell and Ted Lucas. But the streets can't be separated from the art, as the rappers and producers from South Florida rubbed elbows with the hustlers from Miami's hoods like Liberty City. Whether it was Zoe Pound or Boobie Boys, the hip-hop artists immortalized these street legends in their songs and made it known that there was another Miami that existed across the bridge. And while the glory days of the '80s cocaine boom and '90s crack trade may be gone, hustlers still generate millions of dollars through music whose street influences continue to reverberate like bass from a donk.

GETTING GANGSTA IN THE BIG EASY

NO

Cash Money Records and Williams Brothers

12

BIRDMAN, THE BIG TYMERS, JUVENILE, Manny Fresh, BG, Turk, and most famously Lil Wayne—all names that jump out when New Orleans' Cash Money Records is mentioned. Birdman (formerly "Baby") and his brother Slim created a huge movement in the '90s with Cash Money and, in terms of rap music, put New Orleans on the map.

Founded by Jean Baptiste Le Mayne de Bienville in 1718 as La Nouvelle-Orleans and known worldwide for its French Quarter, New Orleans is a beautiful city with a rich history and a wide mix of cultures all residing and colliding in one place. As the birthplace of jazz, the city attracts millions of tourists each year for the Mardi Gras celebration and never-ending party. But New Orleans also has one of the most vicious, poverty-stricken ghettos in America. It's hard to see a positive future in an area that has underfunded schools, poor medical care, few jobs, rampant corruption, and crumbling housing projects.

The Magnolia projects, one of the largest and poorest housing projects in New Orleans, was built in 1941. In 1955, the complex expanded and incorporated an additional six city blocks. From 1952 to 1978 under manager Cleveland Joseph Peete, the housing project was officially renamed the C. J. Peete Housing Development—but to this day it is still known as the Magnolia projects. As with other projects, conditions deteriorated during the '80s and '90s as the crack cocaine epidemic stormed the city and violent crime skyrocketed.

In 1990, the New Orleans Housing Authority and Police Department set up police substations in the Magnolia and other housing developments to stem crime and stop the violence. Throughout the early to mid-90s, New Orleans had so many killings that some called the city the murder capital of the United States. The Magnolia projects were also where the Williams brothers, Ronald and Bryan, repped the street to the fullest. Coming up in the hood wasn't pretty, but they made a life for themselves and their families, along with countless others, with their music label Cash Money Records.

Ronald, aka "Slim," was born May 23, 1964, and Bryan was born February 15, 1969. Their parents were Gladys Brooks and Johnnie Williams, an ex-military man and owner of multiple businesses including a bar and a laundromat in New Orleans. Johnnie's bar, "Gladys," became a popular hangout for hustlers, drug dealers, pimps, prostitutes, and businessmen. The family lived in a small apartment above the bar.

A month after Bryan's birth he didn't have a first name and was simply referred to as "Baby." The nickname stuck with him for life until he became known nationally as the hip-hop artist Birdman. In 1975, Gladys died from an illness, and Baby and his siblings spent two years living with their uncle in Prince George, British Columbia, followed by two years in foster care upon their return to New Orleans. After their father found out they were in foster care, he fought a long legal battle and got full custody of his children. The family moved into the Magnolia projects. Living quarters were cramped, which led to territorial disputes among the siblings, but Baby developed a close friendship with his stepbrother Eldrick Wise.

Wise mentored Baby on street survival and moving as a hustler. The lure of the streets was too strong for the youngster. He remembered seeing the finely dressed and jeweled hustlers who frequented his family's bar. He saw that Magnolia was poor and people didn't have much—or nothing at all—and he wanted more. Baby adapted to his environment and hustling became second nature. "We was thugging. That's all we knew. That's how we come up," Baby said in an interview on the *Big Facts* podcast. "The streets became my life. I chose that shit."

With drug dealing came big money, which led to hood credibility and notoriety. It got him fresh clothes and a better ride. "I wanted that," said Terrance "Gangsta" Williams, a half brother of Baby and Slim, in an interview with VladTV. "As a youngster you see your siblings getting money, dressing fly, people respecting them, the girls calling all the time. I want that."

Baby and Eldrick started committing robberies and selling heroin at a young age before they got arrested at sixteen. At eighteen, they were arrested again for drug possession and sentenced to three years at the Elayn Hunt Correctional Center in St. Gabriel, Louisiana. After he served eighteen months of the sentence and was released, Eldrick got murdered. He would be the first of the Williams siblings who fell victim to the street.

Slim was always the quiet, laid-back one, but the influence of his father, Johnnie Williams, was strong; he had a mind for business and thought constantly about how he could make money. To go with Slim's hungry mind for business, his brother Baby had keen hustling instincts. At a young age they put in work in the pursuit of independence. This attitude had been driven into them by their father—work hard, get your shit straight, and then you can play. "I was born with the mind of a hustler. My Pa was one. Ain't nobody taught me nothing. I ain't had no role model in this game. I was my own role model," said Baby Williams.

As hip-hop exploded across the United States in the '80s, different regions adopted certain elements and forms depending on the local culture—Miami had the big bass, the East Coast had breakbeats and a hard edge, the West Coast had a laid-back, funk-oriented sound. Meanwhile, in the Deep South in areas like New Orleans, a sound and style called "bounce music" captured the attention of locals of that generation. Artists like Kevin "MC T. Tucker" Ventry, DJ Jubilee, DJ Jim, Partners-N-Crime, Hot Boy Ronald, Juvenile, U.N.L.V., and Magnolia Short were among the first to make hip-hop with a unique New Orleans flavor.

Bounce music is a call-and-response party style of hip-hop that involves dance callouts that are often sexual. Another name for this style of music was "P-Poppin" or "Pussy Poppin" music. A big part of bounce is shouting out or acknowledging the geographical areas, neighborhoods, and housing projects in the New Orleans area.

"Bounce is really what we did anyway. We just took it and put it in another little form," said Slim in a keynote interview at Sync Up New Orleans. "Bounce is up-tempo records. People like to dance to it. . . . And we do a lot of up-tempo records. Our style of artists that rap, they have a swing to it. What I call a 'swing.'" They sing and they rap. That's bounce music. We try to incorporate that all together to make great records."

At first it was more of a battle-of-the-hoods type of music that represented who was more thorough in dance, style, and fashion. P. Poppin was huge in New Orleans. Baby was already known in the city for his hustling abilities in the Magnolia projects as well as his past robbery sprees with his stepbrother Eldrick Wise, who had a reputation in the city before he was murdered.

Slim was more the brains behind the scene and preferred to let his brother Baby occupy the spotlight. It was Baby's idea to push bounce music onto the national scene. He knew they could capitalize on the sound. Master P of No Limit and Take Fo' Records were already making money with New Orleans hip-hop. Take Fo' promoted artists at concerts throughout the Southwest and Gulf. With only two companies putting out bounce, the Williams brothers figured there was room for them to get into this hip-hop hustle. Baby just had to find a way in.

When Baby was released from prison, he surveyed the local hip-hop scene. He got with his brother Slim, and they studied what was going on and how Master P was doing what he was doing. In 1992 they pressed forward and started their own record label, Cash Money Records. Baby and Slim traveled to nightclubs all over Louisiana to find hot artists to sign.

Before the internet and SoundCloud, getting new hip-hop artists noticed required legwork. It also took tens of thousands of dollars to make and market records that could be distributed to DJs and records shops. Baby claims that by the time he was twenty, he already had made a million dollars in the streets. This spawned rumors that Cash Money Records was launched with street money, which, throughout its long history, led the feds to always be sniffing around looking to topple the empire—targeting another set of Black men who had come up from the streets.

Cash Money's first artist was a local named Kilo G who released the album *The Sleepwalker* in 1992. With one rapper in the game, the Williams brothers continued to recruit others. They were determined to find success and make Cash Money the preeminent New Orleans hip-hop label. Baby convinced his friend, a local DJ named DJ Mannie Fresh, to become their in-house producer. By the mid-90s, Cash Money Records had become a popular independent label and had a strong fan base in New Orleans and the surrounding areas.

In 1995, Cash Money artist Lil' Slim was introduced to a then-twelve-year-old Dwayne Carter at a block party, and after hearing Dwayne rap, he was so impressed with his talent that he brought him to Baby's attention. Dwayne ended up being signed as the youngest artist on the Cash Money label. Carter, who took the moniker "Baby D," was then placed into a group with another young rapper, Lil Doogie, and they were known as the B.G.'z. The name B.G. or "Baby Gangsta" paid homage to Terrance "Gangsta" Williams, whose street pedigree was notorious.

Even Baby decided to get behind the mic—a true hustler making money by any means necessary—and if he could be the one shining in the spotlight, all the better. He originally rapped under the name "B-32" and performed with 32 Golds. Later, violence claimed the lives of popular Cash Money artists Kilo G, Pimp Daddy, and Yella Boi. It was a setback for the label but didn't stem its success. In 1997, Baby D and Lil Doogie renamed themselves "Lil Wayne" and "B.G.," respectively, and that same year Cash Money signed two other new artists, Turk and Juvenile.

The four young rappers were called the "Hot Boys," a name they took from a Magnolia projects street crew that Terrance "Gangsta" Williams was involved with. This new bounce supergroup took Cash Money Records to a new level. The young Hot Boys released group and solo albums that all went platinum and multiplatinum and contained hit after hit. The phrase "bling-bling" popularized in their songs even made it into the national rap lexicon as well as *Webster's Dictionary*.

In the early days, the Hot Boys' raggedy tour bus became an avenue for making drug connects. Terrance "Gangsta" Williams sometimes traveled with the group so he could buy and sell heroin at hotels along the tour route. While the Hot Boys performed for growing crowds, Gangsta moved massive amounts of heroin amounting to $30,000 per stop. When older brother Slim objected, Gangsta gave him $10,000 to keep quiet and another $100,000 to hold for future buys.

Slim ended up spending this money on tour expenses, which led to rumors that Gangsta was investing drug money in Cash Money Records—a claim he denied. When he was later arrested for plotting a murder and engaging in a continuing criminal enterprise, the feds offered Gangsta a three-year sentence to snitch on Cash Money Records and the Williams brothers. He kept his mouth shut and received a life sentence plus twenty years. Keeping it gangsta like a real G.

Gangsta had avoided getting involved in his brothers' hip-hop hustle because there was no fast money in it. He had seen them put in lots of hours to book shows, distribute product all over the South, and market their artists—only to have little to show for it. As he was locked up for his drug game, Cash Money Records signed a $30 million deal with Universal Records in 1998. Gangsta regretted nothing as his brothers supported him and his children financially while he was incarcerated.

They would even call him up while on tour and let him use his prison phone time to talk to celebrities they were partying with. "My time went by with ease," recalled Terrance, though it wasn't without hiccups. When Slim and Baby found out he was dealing drugs behind bars, they cut him off for six months. With the feds looking for any way to bust Cash Money Records, there could be no perception that the label was funding a drug enterprise. They had to avoid anything illegal.

After the Universal deal, Cash Money Records had a highly profitable run from 1997 all the way to 2019. They reinvented themselves and the game and had hit after hit. As artists on their label came and went, Cash Money Records still shined. After the release of the popular album *Birdman*, Baby took the "Birdman" moniker and stayed on top with solo albums, new groups, and remixes. He was a mogul who also rapped and performed.

Every hip-hop artist across the country and around the world wanted to collaborate with Cash Money, which led the roster to expand and include not only rappers but singers who ranged from Lil' Mo to superstar Teena Marie. Cash Money Records also moved into films and books with Cash Money Films and Cash Money Content. Of all Cash Money artists, Lil Wayne was the breakout star. He performed at the Grammys and took home a few awards himself. Wayne also performed at the Super Bowl and routinely appeared on top hip-hop artist lists as one of the best spitters in the game. As an entrepreneur, he became president of Cash Money Records before branching off with his own label, Young Money Entertainment, which introduced the world to future stars Drake and Nicki Minaj.

Terrance "Gangsta" Williams was released in 2022 after serving twenty-three years of his life-plus-twenty sentence when he cooperated with the feds, giving them information on some unsolved murders. This snitching alienated Gangsta from his namesake B.G. and sibling Birdman. When Birdman put up money for Gangsta's legal defense, he had set down rules. His stepbrother violated those rules, and the streets don't tolerate snitches. That sentiment pervaded the New Orleans hip-hop community.

"I had a real respect for Gangsta and the stories I heard about him. That shit leave with me. I have no type of respect for him anymore," said Baton Rouge rap artist Boosie Badazz in an interview with VladTV. "Once you go that route I dismiss you from my legend book and X you out. . . . You stay silent nigga. Some of us gonna make it, some of us ain't. That's just how it's gonna be. You can take that 'Gangsta' shit off your name."

The feds never did pin an indictment on Baby and Slim. Unlike a lot of the hustlers who reached for the fame and the glory of thug life, Birdman left it behind. He stayed focused and achieved great success in the music industry. And in doing so he remains one of the few street legends to move into legitimate business and not end up incarcerated or killed. "I wanted the money and I got the money," said Birdman. "I'm still here. I'm fifty-two. I ain't caught no cases. I survived this shit. I blessed a gang of niggas and I'm happy to still be alive doing this shit."

LOYALTY OVER EVERYTHING
QNS
Murder Inc. Records and Kenneth "Supreme" McGriff

13

THIS STORY BEGINS WITH TWO INDIVIDUALS who came from similar backgrounds but different platforms. One is a former drug kingpin who in the mid to late '80s ruled the crack cocaine trade in Jamaica, Queens, and left his reputation etched in stone throughout New York City. The other was an aspiring DJ who studied under Run-DMC and became a DJ himself as well as a producer, a studio engineer, an A&R for Def Jam Music Group, and a label owner.

There are many stories told about the Supreme–Murder Inc. rise. A false one is that Kenneth "Supreme" McGriff was involved in Irv Gotti's rise—that was all Irv's doing. The media has insinuated that Murder Inc. was funded by Supreme's drug money and was the prime mover the Murder Inc.–G Unit beef, but it was Supreme's situation that led to the fall of Irv and Murder Inc. Records. Irv's loyalty caused his undoing.

Irv's story is interesting. He grew up around hip-hop legends and ran around with a street legend, but it was the talent—as a DJ, producer, studio engineer, and talent scout—that led to his success in the music and entertainment business. His connections to street cats came along because of his talent.

"Irv Gotti is tied to three major dudes/outlets in this story," said Queens native Shakim Bio. "His connection to Kenneth 'Supreme McGriff'—of the legendary Supreme Team—along with his ties to Jay-Z . . . and his connection to Darrin 'Dee' Dean of the Ruff Ryder camp were essential to his success."

"Irv played a big part in ventures with these connections. His story is unique because it's a story that has not been told correctly until now.

Instead of highlighting his success and many accomplishments, the story told about Irv Gotti was one that gave him a 'black eye in the game' or made him look bad amongst his peers."

Irv, who is from the back streets of Hollis, Queens, fell in love with deejaying, cutting, and scratching. His skill put DJ Irv in the spotlight and gave him the chance to make soundtracks for people who were knee-deep in the streets. Irv grew up during the rise of hip-hop and the rise of the crack cocaine era, a flash point at which these two worlds—hip-hop and hustling—collided. And in many ways, Irv played a significant role in this collision.

"When anyone speaks about Jamaica, Queens, and hustling there are names that will forever be mentioned," Shakim Bio said. "You will always hear the names Fat Cat and his crew, Pappy Mason and the Bebos, the Corley's, and the Supreme Team. These are names that will always be mentioned until the end of time because they were ruling when hip-hop was not only birthed, but on the rise."

Queens in the '80s had several hip-hop pioneers and MCs who would help develop the genre—Run-DMC; Eric B.; Kool G Rap; Roxanne Shante; DJ Hurricane; Black, Rock and Ron; LL Cool J; Salt-N-Pepa. There were many more coming out of Queens, and they were all influenced by the same drug kingpins—true *products of their environment*.

"Crack cocaine was taking over not only New York City but practically the whole United States. This was the time where money was made in the thousands in just a few hours," Shakim Bio said. "Crackheads was chasing this ten-minute high and crack was cheap—ten-dollar, five-dollar, and three-dollar vials of crack cocaine being sold on every corner of Jamaica, Queens."

The kingpins had organized crews who worked ten- to twelve-hour shifts like any full-time job and followed a chain of command. They also had a "Round Table" where all bosses would meet and discuss business and problems. They controlled different sections of Queens and some also took work out of town. Fat Cat was said to be head of the Round Table, and the men who sat with him have gone down in infamy as street legends of the highest order.

The crack trade was booming in the mid-'80s. Street crews were becoming well organized with handlers, movers, lookouts, captains, and lieutenants. Everyone wanted in on the hustle and filled various roles in what became a million-dollar machine. Even those who didn't work for

Supreme claimed to be on the Supreme Team. "Crack hit New York in '85. It was so crazy," said "Bimmy"—a Supreme Team boss who supported early hip-hop artists and toured with Run-DMC—in an interview with VladTV. "You watch everybody lose their life. I'm talking about everybody from police to fire department to lawyers to dudes on the street . . . they all would come to you."

The Supreme Team controlled the Baisley projects, which were located off of Guy R. Brewer Boulevard. Kenneth "Supreme" McGriff, born September 19, 1960, organized his crew in the '80s. He put a team together made up of dudes with names like "Big C," "Puerto Rican Righteous," "Courtney," "Green Eyed Born," "Baby Wise," "Jeff Dog," "C-God," and "Black Just," and Supreme's nephew "Prince" was also involved.

"Supreme was well respected," Shakim Bio said. "He may have been small in height and size, but he was a 'New York Giant' in every sense, especially in the borough of Queens. He was a very charismatic and strategic thinker, who networked with others and had a solid place at the Round Table with other heavyweight drug suppliers in Queens."

Supreme was approachable and led others with love and respect, and they loved and respected him in return. The Supreme Team was a heavy household name in the borough of Queens. In short, Supreme looked out for his crew. They all had that look of being fly and paid. Gangsta and hip-hop royalty.

" 'Preme,' as he was called, rewarded his workers well and was loved throughout Queens," Shakim Bio said. "He even organized and sponsored a basketball league, where he and other big drug dealers had their teams with personal team jerseys balling on the courts for the championships and bragging rights at Baisley projects." Hip-hop artists, basketball players, and drug dealers mixed regularly in the neighborhoods of Queens.

Rappers and DJs recorded and performed songs about the infamous Preme of the Supreme Team from Queens. There were neighborhood rappers like the Albino Twins and DJs like Grandmaster Vic who made songs like "Coke Adds Life" to honor Preme and others. This was a time when the drug dealers were bigger than hip-hop. Dealers served as role models for hip-hop artists who dressed, walked, and talked like them and wore the big jewelry that they wore.

"Drug dealers were highly respected," Shakim Bio said. "They had all the money, were flashy, with the swagger, styles, jewelry, expensive cars.

They had all the respect as well as the flyest and finest women. Supreme and his team was on top. They were those dudes." The kings of the ghetto.

Federal prosecution records show that at the Supreme Team's peak in the '80s they made $200,000 a day. With the streets talking the haters and gossipers were abundant, spreading information—both true and false—that could lead to an indictment. There wasn't any secret about Supreme being that guy. With all the hype surrounding him and the team, the police were out to get Supreme and targeted him and his crew relentlessly.

"He was arrested on drug charges in 1985 stemming from when police found over eighty pounds of drugs, eight firearms, and over $35,000 in cash at an alleged Supreme Team stash house," Shakim Bio said. "But Preme got out on bond fighting his case, while the police and federal authorities were trying to build another case, a more solid one. Even when Preme was locked up, he was still running the Supreme Team show. That was the type of man he was. Him and his crew still ran Baisley Housing projects."

In 1987, Supreme was out on appeal bond. He had the best lawyers, so even when he was remanded back to jail by the courts (to plead out and receive a prison sentence from drug charges), he prevailed—Preme's conviction was reversed on a legal technicality, and he was back on the streets on appeal bond again. But in October 1987, the FBI and U.S. Marshals Service raided the Baisley Housing projects and arrested Supreme along with several of his crew.

"Jamaica, Queens, was going through a terrible phase in the late '80s with the crack trade," Shakim Bio said. "Drug crews terrorized the neighborhoods, making its citizens scared and held hostage in their own neighborhood. The crime rate skyrocketed during this phase, 1984 through 1988 were the most murderous years in New York City. A lot attributed to the borough of Queens and the crack cocaine trade. There were so many killings. Turf wars. Innocent people being caught in the cross fire. Kidnappings, robberies, tortures, more murders. All from the crack cocaine trade."

Lorenzo "Fat Cat" Nichols, who was the head of the Round Table, had dozens of murders and retaliation shootings to the point where he even had the mother of one of his children killed for allegedly stealing and spending the money on another man. The coup de grace was the ordered execution of rookie cop Edward Byrne on February 26, 1988, in South Jamaica, Queens. It allegedly came from Pappy Mason and his Bebos crew, who worked for Fat Cat. A gunslinging crew who spoke in Jamaican patois.

"The War on Drugs was at its extreme as the United States sentencing guidelines were reformed," Shakim Bio said. "Federal lawmakers put laws and statutes in place to take down organizations from the leader down to the shoeshine boy connected to that organization. The mandatory minimum was now ten years for just five grams of crack cocaine. Life sentences were being passed out like free government cheese, as a lot of convicted dealers took deals to save their own skin and cooperated for lesser time. These new guidelines also abolished federal parole."

Supreme was locked up at the right time to escape this. He barely missed this big sweep and was able to cop out where they couldn't charge him later for crimes done before. He took a twelve-year federal-sentence plea. Meanwhile, his nephew Prince took leadership of the Supreme Team and—unlike his charismatic uncle, who ruled with love and respect—Prince ruled like a dictator. He stacked more murders than cash and didn't last. What was left of the Supreme Team went down several years later on federal charges.

"Supreme was lucky because he lived to see another day," Shakim Bio said. "There was a bright light at the end of the tunnel for him, while others were caught up doing life and football numbers in prison. Prince and all his guys are never getting out. Their own guys took deals on them and snitched them out."

Time moves things as well as people. While Supreme was away in prison from 1987 to 1993, a lot changed in Queens. The way dealers hustled was different. Old adages changed. There was no longer a Round Table. Other dealers moved in, a new generation with new morals and principles. The mindset was different. Respect and love vanished, and in its place came violence, intimidation, and fear. Move out of the way or get clipped.

Hip-hop music also changed. It went from fun party songs to dance songs to the pro-Black phase to gangster rap. When rappers started rapping about hustling in the streets, other rappers followed the trend, trying to make their art capture what they saw. Their environment was rough, and their videos showed these rappers *livin' the life of Pablo Escobar* as they tried to emulate in verse gangsters like the Supreme Team.

"There was a new breed of rappers who were hard-core and spitted that street shit," Shakim Bio said. "Queensbridge's lyricist Nas even shouted out big brand-name drug lords in his songs like 'Memory Lane,'

'Street Dreams,' and other songs where he mentioned Pappy Mason, Fat Cat, and the Supreme Team. The rappers were still honoring the legends of Queens. There is too long of a list to name all these rappers, but everyone turned gangster or hard-core."

Born Irving Domingo Lorenzo on June 26, 1970, Irv lived in the Queens Village section of Queens that was considered the "back streets" of Hollis. At that time dudes from that neighborhood wanted to be accepted and recognized by their peers, so they considered themselves Hollis residents as well. Hollis was a middle-class section of Queens that bordered the St. Albans section. Hollis Avenue was the main street later made famous by Run-DMC.

Run-DMC was, of course, the rap trio composed of Joseph "Run" Simmons, Darryl "DMC" McDaniels, and Jason "DJ Jam Master Jay" Mizell. Run was also the younger brother of hip-hop icon Russell Simmons, who at that time was promoting rap acts. His first big act was Kurtis Blow, and Simmons later founded Def Jam Recordings. Run-DMC was one of the first rap groups to introduce the B-boy look and style into the mainstream. They wore gold rope chains, black fedoras, black Adidas tracksuits, and Adidas shell-toed sneakers. It was a look they got from observing the gangsters and dealers in Queens.

"Hollis, Queens, also had its hustlers and gangsters who made a name for themselves around the neighborhood and beyond," Shakim Bio said. "There were also known Supreme Team members who came from Hollis. Just walking distance away from Queens Village, the young Irv used to go up on Hollis Ave. He knew all the familiar faces and had older brothers and a sister who he hung around. Going to Hollis Park where everybody hung out was no big thing."

Irv grew up in the era around the rise of the crack cocaine epidemic. He heard the stories of these guys and also saw firsthand how guys from around the way didn't have regular nine-to-five jobs. These same guys wore the latest fashions, top-dollar sneakers, tons of jewelry, and drove expensive cars—so it was easy to see what they were into. Plus crackheads were everywhere in the '80s.

Run-DMC's first album, *Raising Hell*, came out in 1984. They were superstars since they arrived on the hip-hop scene. All you heard on every boom box on every corner, at the basketball courts, in every car that drove by blasting music, at every house party was Run-DMC. Not only in Queens, but all over New York City, and soon the world. But to Irv they were just the local guys who made good, the homeboys, and they represented Hollis, Queens.

They even said so in their songs—*Shout out to the Hollis crew and Hollis, Queens*. Even when LL Cool J came out later that year with his classic hit "I Need a Beat," he name-dropped Hollis, Queens—when in reality he was from St. Albans, Queens, an area that borders Hollis. It seemed everyone wanted to claim Hollis.

"Irv fell in love with the music since back then—he was also able to see these hip-hop legends in the making regularly in the neighborhood," Shakim Bio said. "Many were fans of the lyrics, but Irv wasn't just enjoying the lyrics, the storytelling, or chorus, he was glued to the beats, the bass line, the cuts, and scratches—the music elements that together created this sound. He fell in love with the vibes and reaction it gave to the audience. He learned that the DJ controlled the crowd; an MC was nothing without a great DJ."

All four elements of hip-hop—break dancing, graffiti, emceeing, and deejaying—relate to each other, but emceeing and deejaying go together most. If you're creating a song—and not freestyling or doing an instrumental—you can't have one without the other because they're of course interconnected. The lyrical prowess of the rapper depends on the rhythm and the beat. The DJ keeps the beat, timing, speed, and sound on point so the MC can deliver their lyrics. And if the DJ can't do this, the MC fails to entertain the crowd. It's imperative that the DJ be skillful and know where and when, as well as what to do, when the beat drops. All this is the responsibility of the DJ.

"Hanging around with his older brothers Rory and Chris, Irv was able to be around the Run-DMC inner circle and witness some of the magic being created," Shakim Bio said. "He saw Run rehearsing his lyrics, DMC adjusting his clothes, DJ Jam Master Jay behind the turntables working the mixer. Irv got to hang around and study what real B-boys were. Whatever Jam Master Jay did to perfect his deejaying craft, Irv studied it; he engrossed himself in every detail and decided that this was what he wanted to do. He wanted to be a DJ."

His sister Christine and brothers Rory and Chris all chipped in to buy Irv his first set of equipment: two turntables and a mixer. And from that point Irv practiced constantly and perfected his craft. As time went on, he became "extremely nice" (street slang for being extraordinarily good).

He later formed a group called the "Def Crew," which consisted of MC Romeo and Rahzel.

"MC Romeo was a battle MC who was dangerous with the word-play," Shakim Bio said. "They were a neighborhood group who entered talent shows, and Romeo was known in Queens high schools as a battle MC. No one really paid close attention to the DJ. . . . But Irv was the foundation that made the group sound great."

Romeo later became co-writer of the classic movie *Belly*, and Rahzel later joined Philadelphia's rap supergroup The Roots. Rahzel performed with The Roots as the "human beatbox," making beats with his mouth in the style that Doug E. Fresh popularized in the hip-hop classic "The Show."

"Irv first made a name for himself at a park jam at Hollis Park in '86–'87," Shakim Bio said. "Everyone from Hollis, Queens Village, Murdock Avenue, and all the adjoining areas was there having a great time enjoying the music. While the DJ was doing his thing, Irv played the background. He was present but quiet. He wanted his chance to show all the neighborhood hustlers and hood stars his skills, but since he was a backstreet dude, he probably wouldn't get any play."

But a hustler by the name of Shane "Qasim" Fells, who was known for his boxing skills and getting money in Hollis and Springfield Gardens, Queens, vouched for Irv and told the DJ to let him spin. Qasim was no joke, known to all and feared by many. Irv didn't let him down. He showed out and surprised the park with his skills. He was now recognized as that dude who can really DJ.

"In the late '80s—like 1987, '88, and '89—a lot of guys in the neighborhoods was attracted to the street hustling," Shakim Bio said. "Everybody was trying their hand in the drug game. It was an open market, and all the organized crews of Queens were gone in prison or in the graveyards. Just about everyone was either in the drug game or acting like they were. Driving nice cars with expensive rims, booming sound systems, and wearing jewelry."

DJ Irv was in the mix of all this. He was running with a known crew of street hustlers who were heavy in the drug game. He was there to witness a lot of shit, but not fully involved himself. People knew him only as a DJ—he made custom mixtapes for all the hustlers in and outside the neighborhoods in Queens. He sold his mixtapes like drugs, ten and twenty dollars a pop. He was consistent with the hottest shit, exclusives or whatever, and he made enough to buy a car from his mixtape hustle.

"The crew he was running with at that time were making moves, they were visualizers, who were MCs and street entrepreneurs," Shakim Bio said. "My book, *The Last Illest*, chronicles DJ Irv running with my crew. The feds said we were in different states moving kilos of cocaine and crack. Almost all of us ended up in the feds and state prisons doing football numbers. Irv met a lot of people hanging with us."

The music scene was different back in the late '80s; it was more underground. A lot of DJs were getting attention doing sets in Midtown Manhattan hot spots like the Red Zone where DJ Funk Master Flex spun at on certain nights. Wetlands and the Octagon were other frequented spots. There were boat cruises on which DJs like Ike Love, Baby J, and others were spinning. They were up and coming and hot. Irv worked those same underground circuits.

"He linked up with a Brooklyn rapper named Big Jaz, who later became Jaz-O. Jay-Z started out as Jaz's hype man. Irv went on tour to Europe with them as a DJ," Shakim Bio said. "Irv was establishing relationships with them before they were known. He knew DMX, who was an aspiring battle rapper from Yonkers way before the fame. In 1993, Irv was getting acts where he made sampled beats and engineered in the studio. He had an MC from Flushing, Queens, who went by the name of 'Mic Geronimo.'"

Irv produced songs and got a deal with Blunt Recordings, where he ended up as an A&R. He also had the group Cash Money Clique, who later on became Cash Murder Clique and consisted of Chris Black and Ja Rule. They were doing studio cuts and making videos. Irv already had a vision that one day he was going to be major. It was him, Daymond John, and Harold "Hype" Williams—all from Queens, each having a vision that would change hip-hop culture forever. Daymond with his fashion FUBU, Hype Williams with music videos and later a classic movie, and Irv with his sound.

"It was all in motion in the early to mid-'90s," Shakim Bio said. "Irv was around some ill cats for real before he was around Supreme. Those cats were about that life for real. They were doing stickups and using the money to book studio time to record songs about the shit they were actually doing. Irv made the soundtracks to these guys who were knee-deep in the streets, selling weight, taking over turfs, shooting up the blocks."

Irv wasn't involved in that at all but ran with the dudes who were. He made the music they vibed to and made beats they spit their lyrics over. In 1996, while shooting a low-budget music video with his Cash Money Clique, Irv was in the same neighborhood that Supreme used to run. Unknown to Irv, Supreme had been home since 1993 and happened to be in the area and stopped by to see the video being shot.

"When Irv saw Preme and was introduced to him, he was mesmerized by meeting a living Queens legend, who ruled the streets of Queens," Shakim Bio said. "At the same time Preme was amazed at the changes in hip-hop and how the world now revolved around the culture that he spawned. It was this meeting of the two worlds and two generations that formed a friendship that would last a lifetime."

Irv was making major moves in the music scene. He left Blunt Recordings and was now at Def Jam, home to LL Cool J, the Beastie Boys, Public Enemy, Red Man, Method Man, Slick Rick, and so many others who started their careers at the famous label. Rapper Foxy Brown and even West Coast artist Warren G were on the label.

"The West Coast ran hip-hop at that time and the East Coast was looking to take that back," Shakim Bio said. "With Irv now on board, he was ready to do his thing. At the same time Supreme was back on the streets looking for a better way. He saw that the hustle changed and the younger generation wasn't fearing the 'back in the days' ways of things."

Bio added: "These younger cats wasn't groomed the same, the principles were different, no respect. It was shoot-first-talk-about-it-if-you-live time. Preme needed a better way and seen it through the hip-hop culture. It was now bigger than the crack trade he once ruled. The rap game was the new-and-improved crack game. Preme had ideas of bringing hood novels by authors like Donald Goines to life on the movie screen or straight to DVD."

Preme was learning that lane but didn't have the connections or people in position who knew who was who. And here he meets Irv. In return, Irv meets the guy who all the cats he ran with either idolized or tried to be like. Supreme from the Supreme Team was one of the biggest if not the biggest name in the streets of Queens, New York, in the '80s and now Irv had him calling and meeting up with him.

In 1997 and 1998 Irv proved his worth to Def Jam. Because of him a merger happened between Def Jam and Roc-A-Fella, which brought

Jay-Z to the label. Irv also helped get Yonkers spitter DMX signed to the label. Def Jam was back on top, and Irv was the hottest dude in the music industry with his ability to identify great music and use his connections in the underground circuit.

"His dealings with Supreme was also on another level," Shakim Bio said. "Supreme was still that dude to many and bringing him around gave Irv the street credibility of a lifetime. Hearing the rapper's hustler/ street hard-core lyrics plus being seen with the infamous Supreme of the Supreme Team, what's more realer than that?"

After doing what he did for Def Jam, Irv wanted his own label. Several parent companies were bidding to get him under their umbrella. Interscope was one. Knowing what Irv was capable of, Def Jam and Russell Simmons didn't want to let the homie go. Simmons gave him $3 million to start his new label under Def Jam. Now Irv just needed a name.

"The original Murder Incorporated ruled in the 1930s through 1940s," Shakim Bio said. "They were a mixture of Jewish and Italian Americans from . . . Manhattan and Brownsville, plus the East New York sections of Brooklyn that were connected in organized crime in New York and its bordering states. Murder Inc. were the acting enforcement arm of the American Italian and Jewish mobs. They were said to be responsible for over a thousand contract killings. Their leader was Louis 'Lepke' Buchalter and they counted Abe 'Kid Twist' Reles, Benjamin 'Bugsy' Siegel, Meyer 'The Brain' Lansky, and Albert 'The Mad Hatter' Anastasia as leading members. These dudes were the truth in those days. Cutthroat gangsters who took no shorts."

These organized crime figures fascinated Irv. He was used to being around bosses, and each member of Murder Inc. was a boss in his own right. Irv felt that he could successfully put together a label of bosses. The original Murder Inc. crew was going to include superstar rappers Jay-Z and DMX, but because of creative difficulties between the two superstars it didn't happen. But Irv still had a roster of his own that he put together.

The feds later claimed that Kenneth "Supreme" McGriff was part of Murder Inc.— but he held no shares in it and had nothing to do with any of Irv's successes before the Def Jam deal. He didn't front the money to start Irv's label either. It all came from Russell Simmons.

"It was all bullshit," said Irv Gotti in an interview for VladTV. "It was all bullshit what [the feds] did to me so I wouldn't help Supreme fight his case. They knew I would give Preme the money for his lawyer to fight his case and so it was a chess move to destroy me and take all my money. . . . Forget the government, any idiot can research and see how I got my rise."

"The relationship between Irv and Supreme was Irv trying to help a legend who at first wanted to change his life," Shakim Bio said. "They formed a partnership where Irv was helping Preme with his dreams of bringing these hood movies to reality. Irv even bought the rights to several Donald Goines books from the author's estate to make sure Preme could do his thing, but the thing is with all these good things coming Supreme's way, he couldn't leave those streets behind."

The younger generation moved differently. While some newer-generation guys admired Supreme, others wanted to test him. They didn't care about the "back-in-the-day" shit. Young lions forever try their elders. The law of the jungle. There wasn't no falling in line to what Supreme said. That was that '80s shit. No one was trying to listen to that.

Instead of falling back and bowing out gracefully from the streets for a bigger cause, Supreme felt that he had to prove a point. Things got out of hand and became very personal. The end result was both Supreme and Murder Inc. went down. Supreme was public enemy number one and Murder Inc. were targeted because of their association with him.

"Feds always want to nab the bigger kingpin as the end goal. There's nothing they'd rather do than take down the Enron of the music business; investigating rappers appears to them to be their fastest route to achieving that," wrote Derrick Parker, NYPD "hip-hop cop" and author of *Notorious C.O.P.*

Supreme ended up in a prison cell serving life and it cost Irv everything to remain loyal to his friend.

FROM STREET HUSTLERS TO RAP OVERLORD

NY

Ruff Ryders Entertainment and Darren "Dee" Dean

14

1520 SEDGWICK AVENUE in the Bronx. The place where DJ Kool Herc threw his first party. Living right above Kool Herc in the same building was a Black Muslim family known as the Dean family. The Dean brothers, Joaquin ("Waah") and Darrin ("Dee"), often climbed down from the third-floor balcony to Herc's on the floor below. Hanging out with the godfather of hip-hop inspired them, and twenty-five years later they formed the Ruff Ryders with their sister, Chivon.

Ruff Ryders started as a multistate motorcycle club and lifestyle brand that eventually stretched worldwide and got into music, film, apparel, and other ventures. The label produced multiplatinum-selling artists such as DMX, The LOX, Eve, and Drag-On. They even discovered and guided the career of their producer and beat-making nephew, Kaseem "Swizz Beats" Dean, who rose to serious heights with his music and business sense.

Before Ruff Ryders existed, brothers Waah and Dee were in the streets hustling drugs and handling business in Harlem, the Bronx, and Mount Vernon, New York. Living in the same building as Kool Herc, they would carry record crates for the hip-hop godfather. This access gave them a rare view into the birth of hip-hop when it came to deejaying as well as the other three original elements—emceeing, break dancing, and tagging.

When their parents separated, Waah and Dee moved with their father to Mount Vernon, in Westchester County, just minutes from the Northeast Bronx. If you lived in Mount Vernon, you could easily walk across the street and be in the Bronx. Going to different homes in different areas, the Dean brothers met a lot of kids, many who were already running in the streets. They had been raised as disciplined children in the Nation of Islam, but the influence of their peers in the surrounding hoods started to shape them.

"We were just living life," said Dee in an interview with VladTV. "We knew a little bit of our religion but we were kids. We didn't know the difference." Dee would go to prison after he robbed a KFC and his brother Waah soon followed after he committed a robbery. After doing short jail time, Waah and Dean got involved in the drug trade. The brothers made about $3,000 a day moving crack hand to hand. Crack was the new hustle that everyone jumped into, but few who did came out winners. It was a trap.

The early '80s can be considered the "golden age" of hustling because there was a new, highly addictive product—crack—and during the Reagan Era people had money and were smoking crack everywhere. As a result crime rates skyrocketed across the nation, from the projects to the suburbs—nowhere was safe and the epidemic affected everybody, whether you were rich or poor, Black or white. It hit Black communities hardest, and they became ground zero for the flourishing crack trade.

Waah learned early the perils of the street when a masked assailant attacked him brandishing a gun. When the gun jammed, Waah threw his money and ran as the triggerman clicked behind him. Waah zigzagged to evade the barrage but one bullet hit him and he had to be hospitalized. The bullet couldn't be removed and stayed with Waah as a wake-up call. While he recovered, he reevaluated his life. The money was good in the streets, but the risk wasn't. He had to find a new lane to ride in.

Waah socialized with a lot of people and knew some associates who had switched to the music game. The rap game was the new crack game. Hustlers had broken into a world that they claimed was better and safer than the streets and produced the same kind of money, lifestyle, and vibe. Best of all it was legitimate. You wouldn't end up dead or in jail. At least that was what they thought.

"Hustling niggas, Waah had started to see how much money was being made in hip-hop while him and his peoples were losing lives in the street over much less dough," wrote DMX in his autobiography *E.A.R.L.* "It didn't add up. So one day he made up his mind that music was going to be his new hustle; it was a way to make paper that didn't involve death or trips up north."

There were rappers who had talent but not the business savvy to take it to the next level. They needed guidance, and Waah saw that as his way. He'd gotten a taste of the music scene from DJ Kool Herc and wanted more. Waah had learned the value of working hard to make money from his father who operated a fish import business. Once when Waah went to his father's office to ask for money, his father told him to get some fish and shrimp out of the freezer and try to sell it. When the youngster came back with $300, his father was proud and said he could keep it. To get to the top of hip-hop, he'd put his mind to work and study the music game the way he did the drug trade. For an entrepreneur, the product may change—fish, drugs, music—but the method doesn't. Waah decided he'd go even harder than he had approached any other hustle.

In Mount Vernon, where Waah was living and doing his daily hustling, he saw other Mount Vernon rappers like CL Smooth, DJ Pete Rock, and Heavy D and the Boyz rising to hip-hop stardom. They had gone from riding skateboards and bicycles to driving Bentleys and BMWs. He knew Heavy D from around the way. One of Heavy's brothers hung around Waah and Dee, so they were able to inquire more about the music industry. One day when Waah was out dealing, Heavy D rolled up in a Benz and gave him some advice. Heavy told Waah to find an artist he really believed in and invest all his time and energy into that artist. Heavy said it would pay off. This turned out to be crucial advice for Waah.

And Waah would need all the advice he could get. The music business wasn't as easy as a drug hustle. Dealing drugs brought fast money, especially during the crack era. A small investment in cocaine could yield $20,000 to $30,000 in a day if you had a good drug spot. Music, on the other hand, required investment, groundwork, and patience. But no hustle was easy in the beginning, and sacrifices had to be made. And in the end there was no guarantee it would pay off.

As for setting up his organization, Waah wanted to ride with Dee, but the young man was deep in drug slinging. So Waah brought his sister Chivon into the fold and they eventually built enough management skills to advance the family business. It was important to Waah to keep business within the family.

It took time for Waah to find the new fresh talent he was searching for. He was a street dude, so he wanted a rapper who possessed "street cred." Waah stayed ten toes down, believing his time would definitely come.

Though he didn't yet have a name for his management team, Waah kept his ears to the street, striving to build up a stable of groups and spitters. By 1988, Dee also jumped on board to help his brother build the brand.

The Ruff Ryders name came when Waah was watching the Western movie *Posse* with his mother. She noted how the bandits on the way to a train heist were riding rough. Waah knew it described them perfectly—Ruff Ryders. The name reflected the Dean brothers' mutual love for motorcycles. To ride a motorcycle was a lot like hustling in the streets. It was fast, dangerous, and attracted attention, especially from women. Waah and Dee also saw themselves as rough, made from the tough streets of the Bronx. They were also like diamonds in the rough, willing to ride or die, and this willingness made them "riders." "Ruff Ryders," said Waah; "Ride or die," his mother responded. This would prophetically become their anthem, immortalized in the lyrics of their artists.

Waah knew from watching DJ Kool Herc that the foundation of hip-hop was the DJ, who made the music the MCs rhymed over and the B-boys break-danced to. So he built relationships with DJs around New York's boroughs. In particular he hooked up with a young DJ from Queens named DJ Irv, who was making a name for himself in the underground hip-hop circuit. Waah bought Irv his first drum machine so the young DJ could advance his art.

Meanwhile, word spread about a battle-rap MC named "Dark Man X" (DMX) from Yonkers. DMX was from the projects in Yonkers known as "School Street." Waah's friend, William "Tiny" Jacobs, had given the Deans a mixtape that featured DMX, and both brothers were mesmerized at what they heard. They'd found their artist. The handle Dark Man X reflected his presence as he shouted and battle-rapped anyone who had the guts to test his lyrical skills. Not only did he destroy rappers musically, but his background proved he was for real. DMX was a shady character who knew firsthand about shooting and robbing. He had a grimy reputation that people shied away from—thanks in part to his intimidating pit bull he always kept with him for protection. But when he opened his mouth to rap some bars, no one could argue that he wasn't spitting some authentic street shit. It was exactly what Waah and Dee had been searching for.

At first, finding DMX wasn't easy. He didn't come out much during the day, He was a nighttime dude who popped up to do dirt. Too many people were already looking for him for all kinds of shit he did. He wasn't hiding out. He was just not to be found. It took time to track him down, but when Waah finally did it took more time and energy to convince DMX to join the Ruff Ryder team. He had already been sold dreams that hadn't materialized. He was living fast and was already trapped in a management deal.

After days of convincing, he agreed to join Ruff Ryders if they could get him out of his current deal. Jack McNasty, DMX's manager at that time, wasn't really trying to release his artist from his contract. McNasty knew he had a rap star in the making and had invested a lot of time and money in him. McNasty stood firm. He was from the streets and knew what he had but didn't know how to market the rapper. His suggestion that DMX get a flattop and wear polka dots went against the street-hardened rapper's menacing character. Waah considered McNasty to be a "clown-ass nigga" and would use street tactics to secure DMX's release.

One night Waah ambushed McNasty at his house before McNasty could release a massive rottweiler. In the manager's living room, Waah got DMX out of his contract. With the dog locked up in the backyard, McNasty was in no position to make a counteroffer. A settlement was reached with no bones broken or gunshots fired. Dude got gangstered for real, for real.

With DMX's contract taken care of, Dee and Waah booked studio time. Much of their money still came from making street moves, and the loot went toward recording demo songs they could shop to record labels to get a deal. DMX's gritty street style stood out tremendously, but he was almost too real to be marketed as a commercial rap act. He had a bravado and swag as he rapped about his misadventures robbing, thieving, and doing grimy shit. His delivery was mean and to the point. His energy was high—but so was he. DMX was a loose cannon to say the least. He didn't give a fuck. But that was his appeal.

People, including record executives, were scared to deal with him. DMX was still in the streets doing dirt and going buck wild on drug escapades. He'd get locked up. He'd go missing for days, sometimes weeks. Waah and his brother Dee were sometimes back to square one dealing with Dark Man X. They had a struggle on their hands, but they both knew Dark Man was definitely the truth. He just needed some guidance and grooming. The brothers often had to search for DMX to get recording done. They'd hit the crack spots, get him cleaned up enough to get some tracks laid down. Before long he'd duck out again and the process would repeat.

It seemed that the brothers' persistence and devotion finally paid off in 1992. Ruff Ryders got a deal with Columbia's Ruffhouse imprint to release a record for DMX. Queens' DJ Irv produced the single titled "Born Loser," a gritty street record that had a light buzz. Unlike other lyricists who boasted about their fly cars, expensive jewelry, and fresh clothes, Dark Man X spoke about what a dirty fuckup he was. In "Born Loser" he rhymes, *Born Loser, caught up in the game / And I ain't even got nobody to blame.* After releasing the track, X didn't get far. He had no follow-up record, no full album, so after "Born Loser" lost and died, Columbia/Ruffhouse dropped DMX from the label. Ruff Ryders and Dark Man X were a little ahead of their time.

DMX was back on that grimy path he was ever so used to, but one thing that never changed was DMX's hunger to eat MCs. He was still out there destroying rappers in street rap battles. He was known to run around with his pit bull on a linked-chain leash and not only would he battle dudes with his dog on guard, but DMX barked and growled like he was a dog himself. That was part of his gritty style, and he took it on the road. To make sure DMX stayed focused, Waah and Dee brought him to Baltimore, where the brothers were still hustling drugs. X tried to work a drug spot, but he couldn't stand in one place for that long with his toes freezing. Instead, he took on all challengers in street rap battles throughout B-More. Any hustler who bet against DMX lost their money. When not battling, X stayed at the brothers' stash spots writing the illest shit the rap world wasn't ready for.

The Ruff Ryders took DMX all over New York City and out of state to battle other up-and-coming hot spitters for money. He was destroying MCs and cementing his name everywhere he went. The name *Dark Man X* was making noise on the battle-rap circuit up and down the East Coast. DMX also knew other rappers and was appearing on their records. DJ Irv was now at Blunt Recordings with his MC Mic Geronimo, who was also from Queens. DMX was featured on Geronimo's posse cut titled "Time to Build" with two other budding rappers, Ja Rule and Brooklyn's Jay-Z.

There was another Yonkers crew of hot MCs known as the "Warlocks." They would go in the studio and record songs with DMX, who ultimately played the most significant role in discovering them and bringing them to

From Street Hustlers to Rap Overlords

Ruff Ryders. Upon first meeting with Dee and Waah, the Warlocks were being managed by a group called the Mush Men, but they were unhappy and wanted out of that deal. Once again, Waah and Dee negotiated under street terms to get them released. The Warlocks manager said he'd been shot before and wasn't scared of Dee. "You've never been shot by me. Otherwise, you wouldn't be here," replied Dee. While tense, the meeting didn't turn violent, and the Warlocks went with Ruff Ryders.

The Warlocks recorded songs as a group and as solo artists to expand their chances of getting signed. R&B singing sensation Mary J. Blige, also a Yonkers native, passed the Warlocks demo tape to producer Sean "Puffy" Combs, who already had a roster of the East Coast's hottest spitters—gold and platinum rappers plus singers who had landed on the hip-hop charts. Puffy's label, Bad Boy Entertainment, already had a major distribution deal. Puffy signed the Warlocks—Jadakiss, Styles P, and Sheek Louch—after seeing their skills and believing in his vision to take them to the top. Puffy told them the "war was over" and rebranded them as "The LOX." The Ruff Ryders management team had yet another act signed to a major label.

With The LOX signed to Bad Boy Entertainment, the Ruff Ryders were trying to get DMX signed as well. Puffy passed on DMX, believing he was too gritty and cursed too much to market to commercial consumers. Ruff Ryders thought differently. While The LOX were creating songs, DMX continued making noise on the battle-rap scene. DJ Irv still had close ties with the Ruff Ryders camp and had his ears in the underground music scene. He was instrumental in the merger between Jay-Z's Roc-A-Fella Records and Def Jam. Irv also knew all about DMX because he was involved in his first record. Irv was also involved in the Ruff Ryders putting up money for the legendary rap battle between Jay-Z and DMX.

The mythical battle started out in Harlem with Sauce Money, Original Flavor, Jay-Z, DMX, and others who went head-to-head, bar for bar. When the smoke cleared only Jay-Z and DMX were still standing on the pool table that served as a stage. The battle was unforgettable. There are many different opinions on who got out better or who the winner actually was, Jay-Z or DMX. Shit got so heated that the battle ended with weapons allegedly being drawn. This battle put both MCs on top of the underground rap-battle circuit. No known recordings of DMX were made because he was still unpublished and Ruff Ryder didn't want his battle raps leaking on mixtapes. If one did pop up it would be worth a million dollars. Jay-Z went on to release his classic album *Reasonable Doubt,* while DMX was featured on numerous songs, here and there, keeping his buzz going, but he was still in the trenches doing crime.

One of DMX's crime crusades involving a stolen jacket resulted in a vicious beatdown that left him hospitalized with a fractured jaw. At the time Irv had come up and was now an A&R at Def Jam assigned to find new artists. Def Jam had early success with groups like Run-DMC, LL Cool J, and the Beastie Boys, but in the '90s they were struggling to keep up with the times as challengers sprung up on the West Coast and in the Dirty South. Irv had to bring the heat back to New York and East Coast music and put Def Jam back on top. He believed in Dark Man X and urged Def Jam executive Lyor Cohen to listen to his tape. Cohen kept overlooking Irv's request. His request turned into a demand until Irv threatened to quit Def Jam. Cohen gave in and grudgingly agreed to take a look at DMX. He went with Irv to Yonkers to check out this Dark Man X character.

What Lyor Cohen witnessed was something he'd never seen or heard before. DMX showed up to the studio late and went in with the look that made him the "hood" personified. The rappers who were there battling and showing off their skills cleared the floor so he could take center stage. DMX had just been released from the hospital that day and he spit whole songs through his teeth, which only made his gritty style more intense and hungry. In the middle of the performance, Cohen jumped up and yelled out, "DMX is the man!" The Def Jam executive was amazed to find out that DMX's mouth was still wired shut and signed him immediately. The Ruff Ryders management team had made another major power move.

Ruff Ryders had two acts, The LOX and DMX, signed to two different major labels. They were on their way. DMX left his mark on every song he was featured on, from The LOX's "Money, Power & Respect" to Mase's "24 Hrs. to Live" to LL Cool J's "4, 3, 2, 1." The LOX shined as well with their lyrical performance on Puff's *No Way Out* album and their debut LP. Both acts were getting booked heavily, doing shows nonstop, and getting the covers of all major hip-hop magazines. With their artists' success, Ruff Ryders could move away from street hustling to concentrate full-time on the music. They bought recording equipment, built a studio, got office space, and hired staff that included engineers, producers, and promotion teams. Their nephew "Swizz Beatz" was put to work making beats. At the top Waah and Dee kept their honed hustling mentality, and the Ruff Ryders brand started becoming a hip-hop fixture.

DMX came out with the smash hit "Get at Me Dog," which reached the Billboard charts and rocked the hip-hop world. He became one of the hottest and most sought-after rappers during that time. In 1998, DMX became the first major rapper on a major label to release two full albums in the same year, *It's Dark and Hell Is Hot* and *Flesh of My Flesh, Blood of My Blood.* Both were loaded with hit singles and debuted at the number-one spot on the Billboard charts.

He even had a smash hit single titled "The Ruff Ryder Anthem" that put a face—DMX's—to the team that had become a movement and lifestyle in hip-hop. The music video showed the Ruff Ryders as an army composed of street thugs, motorcycle/ATV riders, other rappers, and pit bulls all under one banner—the "R" emblem. Dark Man brought the "ruff" to the group as he rhymed. The LOX showed up making their appearance in the video screaming "Ruff Ryders" along with DMX, which made the movement take off. From the streets to the mainstream.

DMX's records sold millions and went multiplatinum. The LOX album hit gold status. With a certified hit artist and group, Waah knew they were ready to take the movement to the next level. It was time to move from being a management venture to a full-fledged record label. Waah, Dee, and sister Chivon founded Ruff Ryders Entertainment and signed a deal to operate as a subsidiary of Universal Music Group. The management company started its own sublabel under Interscope.

Ruff Ryders was now an international brand that not only managed artists; they were about to put out records. They had come a long way from hustling crack cocaine in the streets. Ruff Ryders signed some of the hottest spitters to their label and hot producers such as Dame Grease and P. K. The studio was open twenty-four hours a day with each producer working an eight-hour shift, a business policy the Deans borrowed from their drug hustles. The production team of course included Swizz Beatz. Swizz and DMX became friends and spent time running the streets robbing, jumping cabs, knocking over delivery men, and getting into whatever trouble they could find.

The label put out numerous albums, including *Ryde or Die Vol. 1,* a compilation album that featured DMX, The LOX, and Eve. They followed that with *Ryde or Die Vol. 2, Ryde or Die Vol. 3: In the R We Trust,* and finally *Vol. 4: Redemption.* Eve, who was known as the first lady of Ruff Ryder, a female MC from Philadelphia, called herself the "pit bull in a skirt" and released three full albums for the label. Ruff Ryders were headlining their own national and international tours. In addition to Eve and The LOX, the company had Fiend, Drag-On, Swizz Beatz, and Parle signed to their roster and still had DMX repping as well. Ruff Ryders started producing thug workout DVDs, clothing for dogs, apparel for the streets, hats, tank tops, and official motorcycle gear.

Their Ruff Ryder motorcycle club had some top stunt specialists like "Winky Wink" riding with them and went worldwide. The Ruff Ryders were organized like a biker club, with three hundred chapters worldwide. In the United States, the club was repping in every state, rolling a thousand deep and showing up heavy wherever Ruff Ryders artists performed on tour. "We come from a family-based situation. When you become a Ruff Ryder, you become a family member. And once you become family you become part of the movement," said Waah. "It's a beautiful thing."

While the Dean brothers successfully moved away from street life, DMX kept getting pulled back into it. His fame and money only fueled more drug binges. He got charges constantly and his rap sheet grew longer. DMX had once rapped, "I sold my soul to the devil and the price was cheap." It wasn't a contract he could get out of as easily as the one he had with McNasty at the start of his career. To hear him tell it, Dark Man X was a demon who needed to be fed a steady diet of street antics—from robbing to fighting—and all under the influence of crack. Later in his life DMX attempted to go straight, became born again, and even tried preaching during one of his bids. Despite the efforts to repent, DMX was found dead of a cocaine-induced heart attack in a hotel parking lot on April 9, 2021. He was fifty years old. The devil had finally cashed in on that contract.

Even with the fame, money, and success, the Deans never lost their hustling spirit. They stayed true to their roots, and Ruff Ryders Entertainment is now regrouping to step back into the hip-hop scene with fresh new artists. Their story—captured recently in a documentary series on BET—is a famous one that took place because of the focused determination of New York City hustlers. Two brothers and their sister. "How we was able to impact the music industry in this magnitude is because we came in as a family," said Dee. It was a family that grew to thousands—the Ruff Ryders. Wherever grimy beats, dog barks, and motorcycle roars, their anthem can be heard loudly—"Ryde or Die."

A PHILLY GANGSTER GETTING OUT OF THE GAME

PHL

Take Down Records and Ace Capone

15

THE CITY OF PHILADELPHIA HAS HAD SEVERAL successful hip-hop stars from the '80s to the present day—Schoolly D, Steady B, Cool C, the Hilltop Hustlers crew, Tracey Lee, The Roots, Eve, Beanie Sigel, Freeway, State Property, Young Gunz, AR-Ab, Cassidy, and Meek Mill, to name just a few. Ace Capone wanted to be the next in that long line. Like many hustlers before him, he wanted to succeed in the music game and leave the illegal street activities way behind him. He had visions of grandeur for himself and his rap career.

"Everything was going beautiful for Ace Capone," Shakim Bio said. "He was rich. He made it out of the hood of West Philadelphia. He owned a record label, an entertainment company, expensive cars, a beautiful home in the Delaware suburbs, had a beautiful girl and family, he even had a movie out that he produced. Just as he thought he was done with the drug game and on to real success, everything went wrong."

Alton Coles, who was a part of Philadelphia's large Muslim community, was known as Naseem, but he also went by the name "Ace Capone." At twelve years old, his mother abandoned him and his siblings, split them up, and passed them around from one family member to another. Eventually Ace Capone landed in the rough streets of Philly with an aunt and later his grandmother. "I lived on the block . . . where everything is going down. I started being influenced by what was around me, man," said Ace Capone in a call from prison for an interview with *Philly F.A.M.E.* "That's when I started getting in trouble. I had a no-care attitude toward life. I felt like, *Ain't nobody want us so I'ma do me. I'ma do it my way.*"

These streets were the same ones the Black Mafia ruled in the '60s and the '70s and the ones Junior Black Mafia ruled in the '80s. Alton Coles took the name Ace Capone from the gangster Al Capone. He started from the bottom and worked his way up to the top, ruling Philly in the late '90s until his 2005 arrest. His was a $25 million network that sold over 1,200 kilos of cocaine, 600 of it crack cocaine, with allegedly twenty-one shootings and seven murders tied to his crew. That was the government's story at least. Ace Capone knew that nothing in the drug game lasted forever. Everyone had their run. It was all about what you did with it. He was making big money, but he knew that he could get even more money doing something that he loved that was legitimate.

Capone started promoting up-and-coming acts, rappers, and singers. He put on weekly parties on Friday nights at the Palmer Social Club and staged concerts—including one billed as a "Hip-Hop Explosion"—at Philadelphia's Spectrum arena. His brother was a talented singer who couldn't get any label attention. Capone wondered how much money it would take to start a label. His brother suggested that Ace had enough to pull it off. Ace was surrounded by talent in Philly and knew he was the man to showcase it. "I went around and started grabbing all the hot artists from the area," said Capone to *Philly F.A.M.E.* "I rented some studio time down South Philly . . . I basically throw them in the booth and these little niggas rap for four, five hours, man. They crushin'. I said, 'I'm gonna sign them all. We gonna start a label.'"

Capone partnered with Timothy Baukman, aka "Tim Gotti" (aka "Tauheed"), to form Take Down Records—a name borrowed from the dog-fighting world. They signed rappers Bugsy and Snake, who came out with "Streetz Incorporated" in 2002 plus "Scratchin & Surviving," "Alright OK (Get the Point)," and the "Take Down Compilation." Around 2001, Ace's budding indie label caught the attention of Barry Michael Cooper, the writer for hood classics *New Jack City* and *Above the Rim*. Barry was interested in doing a reality TV series for UPN based on Ace and his crew of artists.

Ultimately the project was canceled for being "too real" for TV. Unfazed, Capone pressed on and continued to seek an inroad for him and his team. He thought of the idea of remaking hood classics to promote his artists. He teamed with director Jamal Hill, then a film-school student, to make a straight-to-DVD movie called *New Jack City: The Next*

Generation. Ace Capone wrote, produced, and made an appearance in the 2003 film. It was a low-budget movie compared to the original classic but was bustling with plenty of action that followed the rise and fall of a Philadelphia drug kingpin. It was shot in the hood over a weekend with his artists and regular people with the goal of making it look as real as possible. In the end, it proved to be too real.

The buzz from the promotional film grew as it moved from Philly to the rest of the country and even overseas. A battle rap included as a bonus feature had rappers from other states wanting to take on Take Down. But the dramatic portion also attracted attention and street gossip. Ace had wanted to use real cocaine and not sugar or flour as he saw in other shows. This led to people saying they had used real cocaine. The feds even picked up on this, and the film, which was meant to introduce Take Down to the world, introduced them to law enforcement. "He was already living that life when he made that movie," said Jon Hageman, spokesman for the Philadelphia office of the ATF. Capone saw it differently: "We just brought the raw and realness and it just got blown out of proportion."

Capone now carried the reputation of being a record-label owner and movie producer. He was living life and driving a $200,000 Bentley. He had successfully navigated his way out of the drug life into a legitimate lane. But as his buzz and notoriety rose, he became a target of law enforcement and was caught a couple of times in possession of a firearm and arrested. Capone kept a firearm on him or around him because growing up in West Philly and being poor, he knew that there were wolves who prey on those not ready in the streets. He was once one of those wolves. No one is ever free from being tested or getting got. He had a reputation when he was in the drug game, and he still stayed solid all the way around the board in the music industry. He didn't create the trap; he just survived it and even thrived in it.

Law enforcement raided various homes and stash houses of Capone's associates and found money, drugs, drug paraphernalia, and weapons. They discovered that Capone had real-estate holdings that were listed in the names of women. Cars were also listed in their names, including Cadillacs, Jaguars, BMWs, and several brands of SUVs. When they raided Capone's residence on the outskirts of Delaware, they found large sums of money throughout the house as well as firearms.

The feds indicted Ace Capone on 194 counts along with 22 codefendants. The government put them together because of a link that connected them to one another—however, this link didn't necessarily have to be connected to *something illegal* and had to exist within a five-year time frame. Ace went the distance with a jury trial. Circumstantial evidence and hearsay testimony from a cooperating witness trying to get a deal led to a guilty verdict. Capone broke down in the courtroom as the judge read out his sentence—life plus fifty-five years.

"I don't think no man deserve a life sentence," said Ace. "Coming from our circumstances. I was a young kid; I was rebellious; I was misguided." The feds say that he distributed drugs in New Jersey, Pennsylvania, Maryland, and Delaware and used his record label as a front for a lucrative and violent cocaine empire. He was found guilty of conspiracy to distribute cocaine and with heading a continuing criminal enterprise that engaged in drug trafficking, conspiracy, wire fraud, money laundering, and weapons offenses.

It took hundreds of hours of surveillance, thousands of wiretapped conversations, numerous undercover drug buys, and the testimony of more than a dozen cooperating witnesses to make the case against Ace Capone. The feds went all-out against a man who claims he was out of the life and doing everything legit. Ultimately Capone's story is a footnote in the history of the "War on Drugs" and how it brought down Black men who tried to be successful and move on from how they started. In America, the Kennedys, to name one example, were allowed to elevate themselves through nefarious or questionable means and they are treated like royalty; but let a Black man try it and it's a whole other matter.

"We are very grateful that the jury reached this verdict," Assistant U.S. Attorney Richard Lloret said. "This gang was responsible for about a hundred thousand individual doses hitting the streets each week over a seven-year period." The feds were convinced they got their man. But it really didn't matter if Ace was guilty or not. He was the target of the operation, and the feds always get their man. They pride themselves on their 99.5 percent conviction rate.

"The government got a lot of people into a big case and created a conspiracy that don't exist," Capone said. "These are serious charges, but I'm not the guy that they allege me to be. I'm not no boss of a street organization running a big, giant drug conspiracy." Whether Capone is guilty or not, a close source who was locked up with him said that "Nseem" is a devoted Muslim who is definitely on his deem. He stays in the law library working on his case.

"The feds had him recorded on wiretaps on his chirp phone, which is illegal for them to do to begin with. They broke the law to get anything on him," said the source. "He won his appeal and was supposed to get back in court to give that time back. Despite his incarceration he wrote and published a book, *Go Hard: The Takedown of Ace Capone*." The book chronicles the rise and fall of his record label.

"This book was not written to glorify the game. It was written to reveal the aftermath of what happens as a result of being raised in an environment [with] poor parenting skills, as well as being a key player in the streets," Capone told AllHipHop. "Although the book is solely for entertainment purposes for the readers, the overall gain and lesson of this book is to learn from our mistakes and to lead those who are misled/misguided."

Ace Capone remains incarcerated today.

PART 4

2010s
New Era
Gangstas

WINDY CITY RAPPERS AND DRUG LORDS

CHI

1st & 15th Entertainment and Charles "Chilly" Patton

16

THE "WINDY CITY" OF CHICAGO, ILLINOIS. The Midwest. A city filled with gangsters dating way back to the Al Capone days. But present-day dangerous gangs like the Gangster Disciples, Vice Lords, Blackstone Rangers, El Rukns, Four Corner Hustlers, and many more rule the streets and go to war all within one city. It's like the gangs from Prohibition.

The city is one that is known for being the home of Minister Louis Farrakhan of the Nation of Islam, for being the home of the Chicago Bulls and the greatest basketball player ever in Michael Jordan, and for being a Mecca for hip-hop culture and gangs.

Chicago has brought its share of artists to the national hip-hop arena. There was Crucial Conflict and Tung Twista and his crew, the Speedknot Mobstaz, Ludacris, and Da Brat. Chicago also claims producer-turned-rapper-turned-designer Kanye West. Conscious rapper Common also reps the Windy City.

Also from this city is the lyricist Lupe Fiasco, who tells stories with his melodic poems so uniquely. Lupe's struggles growing up on the West Side of Chicago and his rise to stardom have been well publicized, but what hasn't been talked about much was his partnership with a man who later got arrested and labeled as one of Chicago's major heroin dealers. A man busted with thirteen pounds of heroin who ended up getting forty-four years in prison.

Once upon a time, Charles "Chilly" Patton, Lupe's friend, mentor, and cofounder of their company, 1st and 15th Entertainment, sat next to the West Side native Lupe Fiasco at the Grammy Awards in LA, but now he's in a prison cell. Prosecutors claimed that Chilly and his wife Inita Patton were running a drug enterprise, selling pounds of heroin. They said Chilly was the mastermind of a drug conspiracy that used cell phones and coded language that police tried to decipher on wiretaps. It seemed like another example of a Black man on the rise being taken down.

Patton and Lupe Fiasco, who was born Wasalu Muhammad Jaco, started at 1st and 15th Entertainment in 2001. It wasn't until 2003 that Patton was arrested, when law enforcement found him in "constructive possession" (i.e., in "active" but not "physical" control) of 6 kilos of heroin valued at almost a million dollars and a loaded firearm. Patton's arrest almost derailed Lupe's career, even though the rapper didn't get indicted.

Patton believed in Lupe and mentored him. He believed in him so much, in fact, that they became business partners and ran 1st and 15th Entertainment under Atlantic Records. The 1st and 15th label produced Lupe's music and Atlantic distributed it.

The rapper initially served as vice president of 1st and 15th but became CEO after Patton got convicted on drug charges. He and singer Matthew Santos were two of the of the label's most recognizable artists. Lupe began rapping in 1996 and was part of several rap groups from 2000 to 2005. He began creating music as a solo artist in his father's basement. His father had lived a storied life and had been a member of the Black Panther Party, an African drummer, and a karate teacher with his own schools. Lupe was originally part of a group called "Da Pak," which patterned itself after the West Coast gangsta music that was blowing up at the time. The group released one single, "Armpits," through Epic Records before being dropped and splitting up.

That experience turned Fiasco away from gangsta rap. He started appreciating the lyricism of rappers like Jay-Z and Nas, which moved him into the "conscious hip-hop" movement. Instead of rapping about being "gangsta," he wanted to focus on social issues like education, literacy, and poverty. He worked on a demo with a track titled "Coulda Been" that caught the attention of Arista Records. Fiasco later signed a solo deal with Arista but got dropped when the label fired president and CEO L.A. Reid.

It was during his brief time at Arista that he met Def Jam president Jay-Z. The two became friends and Jay-Z helped Lupe land a deal with Atlantic Records. "We had the opportunity to build up our company or build up his some more. Me and my partner Chilly decided to build up our company, you know what I'm saying," Patton said. While he worked on his debut solo album, Lupe released a three-volume mixtape series *Fahrenheit 1/15* in 2005–2006 on the internet. The first tape includes the song "Welcome Back Chilly"—which uses Mase's "Welcome Back" beat—and shouts out Lupe's love for his partner who just returned from jail after a fourteen-month bid. Cases against Patton would fall apart; he was a master at working the system and manipulating it to his advantage.

The early buzz was crazy. Lupe remixed versions of popular songs to create his own version. In the second tape he took Kanye West's "Diamonds from Sierra Leone" and turned it into "Conflict Diamonds." On his remix version he pointed out the underside of the diamond business. The song caught West's attention, who in return sought Lupe out to ask him to perform on the song "Touch the Sky" for his *Late Registration* LP.

Lupe grew to stardom and garnered Grammy nominations after he released his debut album, *Food & Liquor*. His opening single was "Kick Push," a nod to skateboarding, which was a rarity in hip-hop. With his major releases, Lupe avoided references to criminality, coming across as something of a nerd in studious glasses. Despite the cleaned-up image, his mentor Charles "Chilly" Patton stood by his side from beginning to end. Despite law-enforcement scrutiny, Chilly had allegedly worked his way up to the top of Chicago's drug industry, and even negotiated with Nigerians for his heavy heroin supply, flooding the city of Chicago.

"There is a large amount of money that he received from the sales of heroin. And he was able to start up a record company," said Assistant State's Attorney Patrick Coughlin. Patton and his wife Inita were charged with running a drug enterprise that supplied more than 900 grams of heroin to addicts. Prosecutors claimed that the large amount of money he received from the sales of heroin made him able to start up the record company. They also claimed that he used profits from the record deals from 1st & 15th Entertainment to buy bigger shipments of heroin. Investigators believed that Patton, before his 2003 arrest, had been dealing drugs since the late '80s, years before he and Fiasco began their music careers.

Patton's lawyer presented him as a family man and successful businessman from Chicago's West Side who was being targeted because of his braided hair and hip-hop affiliations. The prosecution's key witness was a drug dealer named Torrick Hall, who claimed that Patton was his supplier. Prosecutors claimed that Patton's wife Inita Patton had rented a storage unit in the southern suburb of Glenwood where police found over 6 kilos of heroin. Police said they found the key to the storage unit as they conducted a May 2003 raid on Patton's home. Inita Patton said that she allowed a friend to store furniture in the unit and didn't know drugs were in it.

Investigators said they had wiretapped Patton's cell phones and had heard him set up drug deals. They also said that police had listened in on a phone conversation between Patton and Jerry Warren, who had a prior drug conviction and who was being surveilled when he picked up drugs from Patton. Authorities pulled over Warren's pickup truck and found a plastic bag containing drugs but allowed him to leave. In a taped conversation played to the jurors, Warren expressed dismay after they let him leave without incident. "For them to take this [the drugs] and not do nothing? Let me ride?" Warren asked. "Something's not right," Patton replied in the recording.

There were no clear connections between Lupe Fiasco and the drug ring. What existed were recorded conversations of Patton and Fiasco discussing splitting up "whole yellow and whole red ones." Even though a witness testified the colors referred to ten-dollar packets of heroin, Fiasco testified that it referred to mixing and prepping music tracks. Patton's lawyers claimed that he was a music producer only, and others in the industry backed that up.

"Mr. Patton has played a crucial role in the development of Lupe's career," Craig Kallman, chairman and CEO of Atlantic Records, wrote to the court. "Through his invaluable knowledge, advice, and guidance, Lupe has developed into one of the most refreshing artists in hip-hop music."

Nine other people, including Inita Patton, were charged in the case. Of those, one was acquitted. The others either pleaded out or were convicted, according to court records. "I love Charles. I am deeply saddened by his circumstances and will stand by him and his family no matter what occurs," Fiasco wrote to the court. Charles "Chilly" Patton was convicted and sentenced to forty-four years in prison in 2007. While Patton was convicted, prosecutors couldn't present evidence to link the drug charges to 1st and 15th Entertainment. Fiasco recorded the song "Free Chilly" in support of his friend. It appears on his second studio album, *The Cool*.

In 2009, Fiasco announced that he would fold 1st and 15th but still stand by Patton and his family no matter what. When Inita Patton got out of prison about 2013, she initiated divorce proceedings against Chilly and filed a lawsuit against Lupe, claiming he was hiding Chilly's money from her.

"Lupe Fiasco is in cahoots with a convicted drug kingpin, hiding millions of dollars from the drug lord's estranged wife to screw her in the divorce, this according to a new lawsuit," *TMZ* reported. "According to the suit, Patton's estranged wife believes Fiasco conspired with the drug kingpin to move more than nine million dollars into various bank accounts in an effort to block her from making a play on the cash in their ongoing divorce."

Lupe's lawyer told *TMZ* that Inita's allegations were baseless, adding, "There are no secret accounts and no illicit instructions." It's been speculated throughout the years, and even implied by Lupe himself in some of his freestyles, that he was part of the heroin ring and that Chilly took the rap so Lupe could pursue his career. If that's true, then Lupe is only being loyal to his guy. What more could a gangsta ask for?

GETTING GANGSTA IN THE ATL

ATL

Gucci Mane and BMF

17

ABDUL RAHIM SAT BACK LOOKING AMUSED, smiling as he fingered his afro-like beard, a habit he developed since growing it out for the past four and a half years. He likes to pick it out; he is proud of his big beard—a feature of the Muslim faith. Abdul Rahim, who is called "Rahim," has been a devoted Sunni Muslim for close to ten years now. He is humble and sometimes seems pious. He's been taking Arabic classes. But Rahim wasn't always like this—he was known by another name in another world once upon a time.

"Fly Paul" was a hustler who always toted guns because he stayed in shit. He was known all throughout the ATL (that's short for Atlanta). These days he's "Rahim" and doing a fifteen-year federal sentence for being a convicted felon in possession of a firearm, which was actually his third gun case. He started his fed bid at USP Lewisburg in Pennsylvania. He then made it to USP Atlanta, where he was at home in the mix, but then transferred to a medium-security facility, FCI Jessup, located in Jessup, Georgia.

"Fly Paul was that fly wild dude. I been getting to that money since I was a shawty," Rahim said, fingering the ends of his beard. "All the known cats in ATL to this day still know who Fly Paul is." Fly Paul was also in the music industry in Atlanta, running around in hip-hop circles. His last gig, which was his only real legal job, was running a street team for Nick Love, former vice president of Marketing and Promotions for the rapper Young Jeezy's Corporate Thugz Entertainment label.

"Yeah," Rahim said. "I was over there doing a lot of shit. I know a lot about Young Jeezy, who is now known as Jeezy. He knew me very well." When asked about the Gucci Mane–Young Jeezy beef, Fly Paul quickly turned back into Abdul Rahim, the devoted Sunni Muslim. "I stay away from that past life now. I really do. It's stuff like that being the reason why I am in prison now."

Rahim is a lost gem who was right there in the middle of the beef. He knows all about it. It took a couple of weeks before he decided he wanted to tell his story. Every now and then Rahim revisits his time as "Fly Paul." When he does, he relives the gangster life he left behind.

Gucci Mane was born Radric Delantic Davis on February 12, 1980. He was born in rural Bessemer, Alabama, and raised there before moving to Atlanta. He started selling drugs and getting into gangsta life in high school. He took to the streets like a natural and got creative with it. While his competitors sold dime bags and nickel bags, Gucci sold three-dollar sacks. His profit margins were slimmer, but he was moving product quicker, building his reputation and his business.

"Gucci Mane was in the streets for real," Rahim said. "He was sticking people up, smacking up dudes, doing shootings, and selling drugs. He was a good example of the definition of 'trap music,' which Gucci helped pioneer. Before the rap shit, he was moving around in the city. He was really moving around on the Eastside. He was like that." Rahim was now in full Fly Paul mode.

He added: "Now, as for Jeezy, he's from a town called Hawkinsville, about two hours away from Atlanta's center. He came to ATL on some music shit in the city and was introduced to Big Meech of the Black Mafia Family. Now I cannot tell you that he was bubbling on the BMF level. I just knew that Meech was behind Jeezy as far as the music side goes."

"He was very instrumental in Jeezy's early career around 2003," Mara Shalhoup—author of *BMF: The Rise and Fall of Big Meech and the Black Mafia Family*—told the *Miami New Times*. "What he did in Atlanta was promote a lot of parties for Jeezy and helped get his music spread around to all the strip clubs, which is how rappers would make it or break it." In other words, Big Meech actively promoted Jeezy's career.

"I swear it felt like it happened overnight. Things in Atlanta had been one way and then BMF happened," said Gucci Mane in his autobiography. "These niggas were hitting all the hot spots—Club Chaos, Compound, the Velvet Room—and shutting shit down, pulling up in foreign sports cars, buying bottles of Cristal by the case, and throwing around stupid money. Tens of thousands of dollars in a night like it was nothing."

While Jeezy was affiliated with BMF, he wasn't a major player in their criminal operation. And while he was a talented rapper, he wasn't as streetwise as Gucci. "I was out there in the mix," said Fly Paul. "Gucci was known as a drug dealer first, rapper second in ATL. The hip-hop world just knows him as a rapper. The ones making noise that I can vouch for in the ATL was Gucci, T.I. was out there a lil something, and Shawty Lo was the dude that everyone knew made it happen. He was really doing his thing. May Allah bless his soul. Peace be upon him. Shawty Lo jumped into the rap game because he saw how easy shit was."

He added: "Shawty Lo definitely was the truth, but he wasn't trappin' like that. He was moving big weight, units. Now Gucci? He was trappin'. Trappin' is hard hustling, grinding where you do the day-to-day daily operations. Putting in the work by being in the paint. You know like the midnight shift to the early morning. Straight getting to it. You don't have no time to do nothing but pump that product. I'm using other words so you can get a clear understanding. Trap is when you in the mud getting dirty, going hard, no lunch breaks. You eating takeouts in the spot slash drug house, also known as the 'trap house.' Yeah, that's where all that lingo came from. Now, as for T.I., Gucci, Shawty Lo, Jeezy, and others, they all talk that trap talk for sure."

According to Gucci Mane, the trap house was "the type of place where the lights would go out and we'd have no power but we still wouldn't leave the house. Or the refrigerator would stop working and we'd send one of the young boys to the store to get us drinks. Or the stove went out and we'd get someone to turn the gas back on illegally. It was a hangout too. Smoking, gambling, and girls. But when the pack came in, it was down to business."

"Gucci is not the most lyrical dude," Rahim said. "Let's get that out there now. He can't spit like how Jeezy can spit. Jeezy is way more advanced lyrically, but when you weigh up credibilities and reputations on the scale, Gucci outweighs Jeezy in the gangsta category all hands down."

One of the reasons Fly Paul got the name "Fly" was because he stayed fly even before he started getting money "trappin'." Paul was a pretty-boy thug, meaning he was more handsome-looking than menacing. He was light-skinned and had hazel eyes. He wasn't as built on the streets as he is now, but his street cred was legit so it made up for any flaws. Fly Paul kept pretty women around and he ran a street team on the trappin' tip as well as one for the promotion team he ran for Nick Love.

"I had a cool friendship with mixtape king and trap music legend DJ Drama," Rahim said. "He used to call me to get the scoop on what's what. Back in 2004, Gucci and Jeezy was both bubbling throughout the Atlanta metro. Gucci was everywhere promoting his shit, he was flooding the streets with his mixtapes, he was everywhere with it. He was grinding music like he grinded in the dope game, maybe going harder."

Jeezy was "Young Jeezy" back then. He had connections through Meech and BMF. Meech had the city on smash and was in everyone's pockets. DJ Drama did mixtapes with Jeezy, *The Streets Iz Watchin'* and *Trap or Die*. There was this producer who was making some beats, an up-and-coming beatsmith by the name of Zaytoven.

"He had some beats lined up and with moves made the two trap spitters come together to collaborate on two tracks produced by Zaytoven," Rahim said. "It was 'Black Tees' and a song called 'So Icy.' This was 2005. Now know this, Gucci was known in the streets, he was known for shooting up shit, smacking up people on some simple ass shit. He wasn't that likable. He was more feared than loved. DJ Khaled stayed away from him."

Once when Gucci believed a promoter was booking shows in his name and pocketing the cash, Gucci and his boys tracked him down to Big Cat's studio and allegedly assaulted him with a pool stick. This led to a warrant being issued for aggravated assault.

"Gucci was still trappin' in the streets and some of his beefs followed him even when he dedicated himself to just music," Rahim said. "No music producers or execs really wanted to make moves with him. His music was hot, but his reputation was 'Gucci stayed on that goon shit'— that scared people to not do business with him. He fell out with some producers he was working with before. You don't want to fall out with Gucci."

Gucci was showing up to venues booking himself at the time and making promoters put him in the show. They couldn't blackball a goon with ties to the streets like Gucci, and then he did some other shit and got a woman from New York called "Big Deb" (Deborah Antney) to manage him. She had connections in the ATL and New York.

"Jimmy Henchman was supposed to be her peoples," Rahim said. "So that shit got Gucci back in good graces, so when his mixtapes was blazing in the 'A' that was all that was needed. So when those two songs with him and Jeezy was done, 'So Icy' took the hell off. They even shot a nice budget music video for 'So Icy' directed by Lisa Cunningham. It blazed the city, then it was all over the East Coast.

Gucci adapted his street grind to the music world and pushed "So Icy" hard. It would be the lead single on his debut album, *Trap House*, and he wanted to get it heard. It was a staple at clubs and house parties throughout Atlanta that year. But Jeezy didn't share the enthusiasm.

"Jeezy and I were never friends, but during the rise of 'So Icy,' we would occasionally hit the clubs to perform the record," said Gucci in his book. "When I turned down Def Jam's offer, those joint performances stopped. Word was it was because Jeezy had a problem with me."

Eventually, Jeezy would get Gucci blackballed around town, and club DJs began cutting the song after Jeezy's intro verse. "My reputation in the city went from rising star to one-hit wonder," said Gucci.

"Jeez did the 'Boyz in da Hood' thing with Puff's Bad Boy Entertainment and had that Def Jam thing," Rahim said. He could have pushed that single. He was hot, too hot at that point, but he wasn't with it. Whatever reasons Jeezy had for not supporting the song, Gucci Mane took it as disrespect. Gucci was known all throughout the "A," while Jeezy was now on a national level, He may have thought he was bigger than the "So Icy" song.

Gucci Mane took the first shot at Young Jeezy. He dropped a diss track "Round 1" in which he attacked Jeezy's credibility and questioned his authenticity. The song was blazing all over the ATL as well as the internet. There was a back and forth with verses referring to each other in their songs, but it didn't seem that serious at first.

"Gucci Mane was eating, getting booked for real now," Rahim said. "Deb managed the hell out of his career, had him booked seven days a week, sometimes two to three shows a night. He was on fire. Then Deb had Nicki Minaj, and then French Montana, all under the Gucci Mane umbrella. Gucci was doing his thing. Jeezy also had his fame. He was a part of Bad Boy Entertainment's Boyz n da Hood group, but separated himself as a solo artist on Def Jam.

Jeezy had his Corporate Thug Entertainment group known as "CTE" that was his running partners and associates before his fame. On a mixtape Jeezy put a bounty on Gucci Mane's head and dared anyone to bring him the "So Icy" jewelry. One summer night, five masked-up men stormed into a woman's home on a home-invasion mission. That's a forced house robbery. So happens Gucci was there staying the night.

"He seen that he was set up by the dirty chick," Rahim said. "The masked men were armed with pistols, brass knuckles, and duct tape. Gucci already knew that his life was on the line. He was at risk. He was a real street dude who lived that life for real. Gucci stayed with a 'strap' [pistol]. So Gucci did what he had to do."

Gucci pulled out his gun and shot his way out of the house, killing one of the men as the others ran off without getting any of Gucci's jewelry or cash. When the smoke cleared, authorities identified the dead man as Henry Lee Clark III, otherwise known as "Pookie Loc," one of Jeezy's proteges under his CTE imprint. Gucci Mane was arrested and charged with murder but charges were later dropped.

Rahim: "Rumors was floating around as the story changes from streets to cities to states, back around again and it was that Gucci Maine killed a BMF affiliate and is beefing with Big Meech. It had nothing to do with BMF or the drug game. It was a rap beef that turned deadly. What's crazy, what spun the story around was that at the same period, Big Meech got into it with 'The Big Bad Wolf,' Puffy's man and after a shoot-out, Wolf was found dead and Meech was hit in the ass. They took the stories and remixed it when all this shit wasn't connected."

After the incident, Gucci Mane faced a murder charge.

"Gucci's defense attorneys would later allege that BMF was behind the home invasion," *Creative Loafing* reported. "And the DeKalb County District Attorney's Office would say that the FBI was investigating BMF's alleged involvement." But two of Pookie Loc's partners reiterated Fly Paul's version.

"BMF had nothing to do with, not anything, period, the Gucci Mane situation and Pookie Loc," Tarence Bivins old *Creative Loafing*.

"That's not true, totally not true. You can quote me on that," Carlos "Low Down" Rhodesis agreed and added, "Basically, they're just using BMF as a prop," he says. "They're going to use BMF just so they can bring more heat." The biggest gangsta on the block.

"I stayed strapped," Rahim said. "Gucci was about his business. I was too. I wasn't taking sides, but I was rolling with CTE. Gucci knew this. Even though Jeezy ended up being the bigger artist record-selling wise, Gucci put more artists on. Gucci put on Future first before anyone did. The Migos. He put on for trap music. Everyone was invited and in and out of Gucci's studios."

He added: "I don't think Meech ever had a personal problem with Gucci Mane. Meech was getting too much money. Some real shit. When we were on the same yard here in Jessup, we switched MP3 for a few days. Guess what was on that shit? 'Yellow Diamonds' by Gucci Mane. Even Meech knows Gucci is the real thing. You can't deny that."

"Gucci Mane even did a fed bid, was in a USP, no protective-custody shit either," Rahim said. He ain't ducking no problems at all. Jeezy Da Snowman is winning right now. He don't care about that shit. Allah please forgive me for the *fitnah* I just indulged in. I seek refuge in Allah from the whisperings of the Accursed Satan." As Rahim finished, he fingered the ends of his beard, smiling.

HOW GS9 INVADED FLATBUSH

BK

GS9

Entertainment and Bobby Shmurda

18

BROOKLYN WAS ORIGINALLY A DUTCH SETTLEMENT composed of six clearly defined towns. These towns eventually became English settlements that made up Kings County, but over time the townships consolidated and became what today we know as Brooklyn. The original towns—Bushwick, Brooklyn, Flatlands, Gravesend, New Utrecht, and Flatbush—still exist today as the greater metropolitan area of Brooklyn. Over the centuries portions of the towns have existed as independent municipalities before becoming part of Brooklyn as a whole.

The current neighborhoods sit much like the original townships did and have kept their names. In 1894 a referendum made the entire consolidated city of Brooklyn into a borough of New York City, and by 1898 the current borders of Brooklyn were in place. This is the textbook version of Brooklyn's birth, but with some examination a different history emerges.

Flatbush traditionally attracted foreigners who came to America and settled in New York. Folks from the Caribbean started flocking to Brooklyn—Jamaicans, Trinidadians, Haitians, and others. Years later people from Africa, the Middle East, and other parts of the world started calling Flatbush home, settling their families and opening up businesses.

"You walk around parts of East Flatbush in the middle of the afternoon, and it feels like a solid, stable, working-class neighborhood. You'd never know it was one of the most dangerous places in the city, but it is," reports Corey Pegues, a retired NYPD commander from Queens, in his book *Once a Cop*. "Gang culture runs deep in Caribbean communities. Caribbean people love guns. They love to smoke weed and they love to carry guns."

As the different groups moved in, they banded together to survive and protect their families and businesses. This led to the rise of gangs in the late twentieth century. Before that there were gangs all over New York City that formed in the '50s and continued through the '60s and '70s. These gangs were inclusive, territorial, and tribal. Hip-hop culture represented an evolution of gang culture—specifically when a historic truce was made in the '70s—but, in reality, gang culture never stopped. It just transformed and went underground. Some gangs changed course and focused on uplifting their people, inspired by the Black Panther Party or the religious teachings of the Five Percenters. Some gangs fell off the map. Others remained in the game. But gang culture still exists today, strong as ever.

As the birthplace of hip-hop culture, New York City has its own versions and flavors of gangs, even though most of them originated elsewhere. The Crips and Bloods were founded on the West Coast but have flourished in the city, as well as the Midwest's Gangster Disciples, Vice Lords, Latin Kings, and many others. New York has added its own swag to these gangs naturally, nothing forced, just a new twist to the lifestyle.

In the early days New York set the styles for both the street and hip-hop, from LL Cool J's Kangol caps to Run-DMC's Adidas sneakers. But as styles spread across the country and came back, New York maintained its own unique ones. Harlem rapper Cam'ron, for example, was known for rocking the color pink—when it came to his clothes, boots, mink coat, and even his Range Rover. "Brooklyn dudes who were in gangs like Decepticons and Lo Lifes, and that's where the trend of hood niggas rocking pink started," said Prodigy of Mobb Deep in his autobiography, *My Infamous Life*. "Brooklyn dudes wore pink Polo sweaters, purple, orange, yellow. Brooklyn muthafuckers loved Polo when I was in high school. I just kept the trend going in 2003."

Prodigy continued: "There was nothing feminine to the way Cam'ron rocked that style and color, he was just being bold. He stood out and others wanted to follow and the hip-hop community ran with it. Cam'ron and his Dipset comrades, The Diplomats, have a very strong presence in New York. Their Blood movement was expressed through rap lyrics, style, and fashion spread throughout New York City and beyond. Merging gang and hip-hop culture yet again."

Brooklyn has always been known as the borough of kings. A place full of talent and hustle but—in certain sections—one of little opportunity and almost no hope that is infamous for stickup kids, gun thugs, gangstas, gangbangers, and scammers. Sheisty Brooklyn kids getting it any and every day they can, consequences be damned—whether it's a beatdown, an arrest, a prison bid, or even getting killed. The borough has always had that Wild West element. It is also the home of the GS9 clique.

In the '80s, when street culture evolved and hip-hop emerged, every borough in New York City was given a slang name that was known by those in the criminal underground. It was all about who you dealt with or who came to prominence in the area. The Nation of Gods and Earth named their boroughs after Islamic areas. The Bronx was called "Pelan," Brooklyn was "Medina," Queens was "The Desert," Manhattan was "Mecca," and Staten Island was "Savior's Island," later to be called "Shaolin."

"Through the '90s the slang names was switched up, but it was according to what generation you was dealing with," Shakim Bio said. "Every borough had its moneymakers, as well as its shysters, but one borough name stuck since the '80s and never changed; a movie as well as various songs lionized the label. Kings County was known as Brooklyn to most, but to the underground it was known as 'Crooklyn,' Land of the Crooks."

It wasn't until the late '90s that Brooklyn was known to produce a variety of money-getters and moneymakers. Before then Brooklyn was known for its petty crime. Brooklyn back then came with a stigma that always stuck in your mind—never trust those grimy Brooklyn cats. Thugs there were known for armed robberies, snatching gold chains, robbing dudes for their coats in the middle of winter, and even taking people's sneakers right off their feet and leaving them barefooted.

"Brooklyn dudes in jail were known to be the grimiest out of all the boroughs," Shakim Bio said. "Brooklyn thought that they always ran shit. So no matter what generation, the mindset was always there in place. Everything was going smooth until those Crooklyn dudes came around.

That's what Brooklyn was well known for in the criminal underground and underworld."

In the mid to late '90s when Bloods culture invaded every block of New York City, there was always opposition. It was a fact that on the West Coast the Crips outnumbered the Bloods. But on the East Coast it was different—the Bloods outnumbered the Crips. The Bloods' main rivals in New York were the "Almighty Latin King Nation." They had a brutal and deadly war with the Bloods until a truce was made in the late '90s.

After that truce the Bloods started warring with the Crip sets that were spreading all across the city.

"Seeing the gang culture in New York was to know it was kind of unique," Shakim Bio said. "But to see it in the Flatbush section of Brooklyn, where there were so many different cultures of foreigners, and their first generation of American children embracing it just how American boys first joined the Cub Scouts and moved on to the Boy Scouts, then to the military, was shocking. That's how the Crips and Bloods gang culture spread in Brooklyn."

"Most of my shootings were gang-related," said former NYPD commander Corey Pegues. "We had the old-school gangs like the Crips and the Bloods, but we had this proliferation of younger, smaller gangs, too: the Blood Stains and the Outlaws, the Rockstars and the Young Assassins, GS9, the Very Crispy Gangsters, the BMWs [Brooklyn's Most Wanted]. The Crips and the Bloods were bad, but they weren't the real problem; they were older and had at least some sense to them. It was the young gangsters with something to prove."

It was deep in Flatbush where GSC formed. The name stands for "G Stone Crips," but there were also other handles that the gang went by like "Grimey Shooters" and "Gun Squad."

"GSC is a street crew. We in the streets. We do what we do. GSC is active in New York City and all throughout the East Coast. Everybody's like get your cash, get your money," member "P Gutta" told *Don Diva Magazine* in 2015. "GS9, now, is dudes out of the '90s that's GSC; however, we have dudes outside of the '90s that are associated, so they call themselves GS9 as well. As long as you official and you bang with the kid, the kid's gonna bang with you."

The Crip set was well known in the Flatbush area for selling drugs. They dealt and waged deadly battles with rival gangs for territory. Shoot-outs were commonplace, and the gang turned the area into a war zone. The police opened numerous investigations on GS9 for murders and shootings in public places where they would open fire on a crowd indiscriminately.

"They were ruthless and reckless gun-toting youths who would empty the clips of their semi and automatic assault weapons on a whim," Shakim Bio said. "They were known to wild out, but that's not the only thing that the GS9 were known for. They were also known as a creative and talented rap group who made songs over other artists' instrumental tracks. They remade their own version, retitling the song, and putting out mixtapes to the streets."

The known GS9 members were Bobby Shmurda, Rowdy Rebel, and Corey Finesse. Hip-hop music was a culture that affected everyone. Music can hype you up. It can change your emotional feelings and all. It was a lifestyle to the young gang members, and they used rap to express not only who they were but what their lifestyle was like. If you want to see what GS9 was about, just take a glance at Bobby Shmurda's lyrics in "Hot Nigga":

I been selling crack since like the fifth grade
Really never made no difference what the shit made
Jaja taught me flip them packs and how to maintain
Get that money back and spend it on the same thang

Bobby Shmurda was born Ackquille Jean Pollard on August 4, 1994, in Miami to a Jamaican father and Bahamian mother. He moved to East Flatbush with his mother after his father got locked up. Shmurda's right-hand man and fellow MC, Rowdy Rebel, was born Chad Marshall on November 24, 1991, in Brooklyn. His father was a known Jamaican gangster. They both came from a line of infamous Jamaican "badmen," which means their fathers were players in the Jamaican criminal underworld.

"With no father, or guidance, they both ran the streets doing what young gun-toting gangbangers do," Shakim Bio said. "But they had something, and if they used their intelligence and played the chessboard correctly, with the aim to win and not just be seen and heard, they could have made it, because they possessed the gift of rap."

There were other crack hustlers who'd made it out from the slums of Brooklyn to the top of the world without looking back, such as Jay-Z. But everyone can't be Jay-Z. That doesn't mean that you can't make it out, though. They came from the very same streets that Jimmy Henchman came from, so just seeing his mistakes from a few years before should have showed them that it's hard to play the street game as a Black man in America and win.

"But when you have a talent that can take you to another bigger level. When you have a gift, something that can get you, your family, friends, and loved ones out of the conditions of being poor, you have to use it to the fullest," Shakim Bio said. "Sometimes you have to leave certain characteristics, lifestyles, and habits behind. Look at Ice Cube, who came from the streets and started N.W.A."

Bio continued: "[Ice Cube] moved on to bigger levels of entertainment, where he's now a mogul. . . . He left a lot of things that would have held him back behind him. His priorities and responsibilities changed. Too many depended on him, and he couldn't let them down. Sad to say, GS9 couldn't do that."

GS9's first song was a remake of Crime Mob's single "Knuck if You Buck." They made a video for that song. It didn't get any real response, but they were recognized for their rapping. It wasn't until Bobby Shmurda used an instrumental track to do another remix that shit jumped off for the crew. He used G-Unit rapper Lloyd Banks's track "Jackpot" to record his 2014 song "Hot Nigga." He made a video in the spring of 2014 that went viral. That's when the GS9 kicked in the door—the song exploded.

Bobby Shmurda presented himself with his trademark smile and energetic dance moves before a packed meeting with Epic Records executives. His viral dance was called the "Shmoney Dance" and involved putting one leg out and leaning over with the opposite shoulder and then switching back and forth. The performance ended with a round of applause and, even better, a signed contract. A radio version of the song titled "Hot Boy" was made and it landed big, entering the Top 100 Billboard at number 6. The song got hundreds of millions of views on YouTube and other social media outlets.

Bobby Shmurda and GS9 became stars when his EP *Shmurda She Wrote* dropped on November 10, 2014. His major label release was slated for 2016 and would be executive-produced by Jahlil Beats, but the album never got released because the GS9 squad were still in the streets, living up to the names Grimey Shooters and Gun Squad. Law enforcement reported that they shot their way in and out of nearly everywhere they went—even their own shows.

On December 17, 2014, nine days after he performed his Hot 100 top-ten hit on *Jimmy Kimmel Live* and just thirty days after the release of his EP, Shmurda was arrested by the NYPD with fourteen others, including his brother Javese and his fellow GS9 labelmate, Rowdy Rebel. Police charged Shmurda with conspiracy to commit murder, reckless endangerment, and drug and gun possession charges.

The *New York Times* reported that the arrests were made after a yearlong investigation into GS9's alleged involvement in various shootings and narcotics trafficking. Police found twenty-one guns and a small amount of crack cocaine during the sweep. But many questioned the timing and validity of the charges. Police pointed to recorded conversations between GS9 members talking in code—with "socks" referring to guns, "crills" meaning narcotics, and shootings called "suntans." They also held up Shmurda's lyrics as evidence of his criminality. For example, the song "Hot Nigga" has multiple references to selling drugs and gunplay. *Hot New Hip-Hop* reported that "Hot Nigga" contained a total of fourteen potential confessions to criminal activity. But Shmurda said his lyrics were "fiction rap."

Shmurda's supporters pointed to the lack of documented drug transactions and said the phone calls were circumstantial. Critics of the bust felt that Shmurda's rising celebrity had a lot to do with the charges and the fact that his bail was set at two million dollars. Shmurda believed he was being targeted because of his music. Law enforcement using a rapper's lyrics as evidence is nothing new even though it's been struck down under the First Amendment numerous times.

"New York cops have a long history of targeting the hip-hop community," Shakim Bio said. "That's something we've seen all across the nation, especially in California and New York, since the rise of gangsta rap. Cops listen to their target's music and their social media and build cases against these rappers off of nothing. Everybody knows about the hip-hop cop cases in the '90s, so none of this should be a surprise."

"That's how America is," Bobby Shmurda told *Complex* in 2016. "They got these kids running around with rape charges getting six months and they wanna give me seven years for a gun charge." NYPD's aggressive pursuit of Shmurda and the GS9 crew, which was described as a violent criminal organization instead of a rap group, bordered on a witch hunt.

"This gang, the G Stone Crips or GS9 as they call themselves, has gloated about murder, shootings, and drug dealing with YouTube videos and viral dance moves," said NYPD commissioner Bill Bratton, addressing Shmurda's case. In 2015, the *New Yorker* reported that NYPD Officer James Essig had said Shmurda's music was "almost like a real-life document of what they were doing on the street."

On October 19, 2016, Bobby Shmurda was officially sentenced to seven years. He accepted a plea deal so that his homeboy Rebel would receive a more lenient sentence. "I did it for Rowdy. They offered me five [years] and offered Rowdy twelve," Shmurda said. "They said the only way they'll give him seven is if I took seven, too. So, you know, I had to take one for the dawg." Shmurda felt like they didn't have a chance if they went to trial.

"They just look at our skin color, and looked at where we're from," he said. "I didn't get caught with anything on me and the cops lied, saying they seen me with a gun in my hand. I explained the whole situation to Epic, and they were behind me all the way. We had big-money lawyers and they still couldn't do nothing because of the judge, who looked at us like Black thugs."

Bobby Shmurda's case is just the most recent one that exemplifies how hip-hop artists can be persecuted in the United States. On February 23, 2021, Shmurda was freed from the Clinton Correctional Facility in New York. His release came ten months ahead of his originally scheduled release date because of good behavior. He'll be on parole until February 2026.

THE MAKINGS OF A MOTOR CITY DYNAST

DET

BMB Records and Brian "Peanut" Brow

19

"I NEVER KNEW WHO KASH DOLL EVER WAS," said Sincere from Newark, Ohio. "I heard her spit on Pusha T's joint 'Sociopath.' I was like, damn, when I heard her. That's what made me go on the JPay music catalog on the kiosk to check for her. She really can rap. Then when I seen how phat her ass was—damn—I just fell in love with the bitch."

Sincere was cutting someone's hair in the day room of Unit 2B at Mansfield Correctional Institution in Mansfield, Ohio, as he reminisced. Sincere was so infatuated that he reached out to the street to ask his people back in the hood what was up with her. Everybody knew about Kash Doll, but not really about her rap skills. All Sincere's homies knew about was Kash Doll's body.

"They told me her label paid for her cosmetic surgery," said Sincere. "She was stacked in the ass and boob department. I was like, damn, what label does that? But my homie told me, 'You haven't heard of BMB Records?' I hadn't, but I quickly learned that Brian 'Peanut' Brown was the man. He paid for Kash Doll's ass and boobs and also was into a lot more."

It wouldn't be out of character for Brian "Peanut" Brown, the president of BMB Records. Before he got into music, he was known for his generosity at Detroit's strip clubs. He even hired a few ladies to act as "BMB Babes" and live in a house with 24/7 webcams in every room. Peanut wanted the best things in life, and he extended this to his artists. If you were signed to BMB Records, Peanut made sure you had the best of everything. He was willing to make his artists' looks match their skills, even if he had to spend money to make it happen. It was part of a philosophy Peanut would later call the "art of sacrifice"; if you lived to serve others first, karma paid you back many times over.

Brian Brown got the nickname "Peanut" because of his small size at birth and grew up on the corner of Cobb and Colfax in Southwest Detroit. Like a lot of the Motor City today, it is a home to vacant buildings and broken dreams. But coming up, it was still a place where children could come and go, playing freely under the watchful eye of kindly neighborhood grandmas and stern block elders. Despite the relative calm, crime was still a way of life. Peanut's father Alphonso was a known robber—even to his friends who were sometimes the victims of his criminality. This brought violence into the home when those same friends retaliated.

Brown recalled that at four years old he went into his family's living room and found a man on the ground crying, bloody, and pleading for his life. Peanut's father stood over the man holding a handgun. He called the child over and pressed the gun into his palm, explaining that the man had come to hurt them and that if they didn't make him "go away" he would return. Alphonso then ordered young Peanut to pull the trigger, but the child—not grasping what was going on and not really knowing yet what a gun was—didn't obey. The beaten man was let go only to return later to shoot up the family's house. It was a harrowing lesson in street life. "When we became grown [my father] still resented me from that shit," said Peanut in the documentary *Living to Sacrifice*. "I didn't have another opportunity with that ever. But I'm certain if he would [have] gave me another opportunity I would [have] made sure that it happened."

Peanut didn't set out to become a drug kingpin, it just sort of happened—because of his personality, drive, and talent for leadership. Growing up he was always the boss, leading the neighborhood children around, even if it meant giving them pocket change for candy and snacks. When his family cut his allowance, he needed to come up with ten dollars a day to take to school. He decided to try selling crack rocks he got from someone in the neighborhood. Because he lacked experience in the drug game, he portioned out his rocks larger than other dealers. He quickly made his weekly allowance money and went on to school. When he came home later that day, he found a line around his block with addicts wanting 'Nut to hook them up. He told them he didn't need to sell anymore this week, but they begged him and he opened up shop.

In six weeks he had made $198,000, which he kept in his grandmother's basement. As the money accumulated, she remembered the piles becoming so large that she had to walk over them to do her laundry. He had been receiving his crack already cooked in what was called a "cookie" that he broke rocks off of. His supplier had been ripping him off by shorting the ounces he received so Peanut switched to a new supplier who gave him a kilo of coke and taught him how to cook it up into crack himself.

His father had given him a beating when he found out his son had broken the primary rule of dealing—you don't keep your drugs and money in the same house. Peanut learned quickly and subsequently worked out of the second floor of an abandoned building. When someone wanted to buy, they would place their money in a plastic juice bottle that Peanut would pull up to the second-floor window by a string. Cash in hand, the crack would be lowered in the same way. He also used marketing strategies like offering a two-for-one special and his rocks were still the biggest around. By using a network of friends and hand-to-hand street dealers, his empire grew, the money exploded, and within six months he claimed to have amassed millions. He was known as a block Robin Hood and was generous to those around it. He put older women up in houses; he drove around and distributed bags of one-dollar bills; and when the ice cream truck came by all the children knew to run to Peanut as he would buy the whole block popsicles and ice cream cones.

The law tried to bust Peanut in the '90s, but he slipped away from the cocaine trafficking charges that the feds brought against him. He got the judge to throw out the charges by claiming he wasn't afforded a speedy trial. The prosecutors were fishing and trying to build a case, but Peanut was just one step ahead of them. The feds weren't done, though. They locked Peanut up again about a year and half later on a different case involving drug dealing.

On June 9, 1992, Peanut was arrested again by the FBI in a sting as he tried to purchase 20 kilos of cocaine from an undercover cop. The FBI found $166,000 cash in Peanut's car—money for the buy. Peanut's attorney was slick, however, and got him released under his care until the indictment came down. But the U.S. Attorney's Office dragged their feet on the case while looking for evidence and Brown didn't get indicted until December 1992.

An arrest warrant was issued in February of 1993, but by then Peanut had vanished. The cops got close once—chasing him by car through a residential neighborhood—but eventually in November of 1993 they declared Peanut a fugitive. His case was handed over to the U.S. Marshals, which landed him on an episode of *America's Most Wanted*. He traveled under assumed names in several states and even lived in an Atlanta dorm and went to school until the cops finally got their man in a traffic stop. But Peanut played the same move that he had before and won. On October 29, 1997, the judge dismissed all charges against Peanut on the grounds that the government had failed to give him a speedy trial and set him free. After fifteen months in jail, Peanut was out of handcuffs again—but it wasn't over. The feds indicted him yet again on January 20, 1999.

As the feds built their case, Peanut paid for a billboard off one of Detroit's highways that promoted a memoir he planned to write about his life. Literary ambitions aside, the feds said his organization trafficked more than 450 pounds of drugs all over the United States. The millions of dollars Peanut generated were used to fund his lavish lifestyle—expensive cars, real estate, jewelry. Over the course of the investigations, the DEA seized $500,000 and 8 kilos of heroin and fentanyl. Despite the seizures, Peanut kept finding loopholes to beat his cases.

The DEA had a confidential informant who claimed that Peanut bought his drugs in California and had direct ties to Mexican drug cartels. But the police didn't really have anything solid. Everyone on the Detroit drug scene knew who he was, though; he was present and accounted for in the streets.

The 1999 case resulted in a conviction and the feds finally got their man. Peanut was sentenced to ten years in federal prison. Even in prison he was a boss among bosses, so much so that the correctional officers often deferred to him and did him favors. One prisoner recalled how Peanut had shared Hennessey and Kentucky Fried Chicken with him in his cell. With his charm and connections, he could get whatever he wanted, including unofficial conjugal visits with his wife Akai as well as a woman named Sabrina, who would become his second wife. With an easing of the harsh mandatory minimums of the '80s came a reduced sentence, and Peanut went home in 2010.

But it seems he didn't learn his lesson and he jumped right back in the game. In 2012, police raided his home on Detroit's West Side, finding one kilo of heroin, three firearms, about $2,500 in cash, and three Harley-Davidson motorcycles. The seizure didn't send Peanut back to prison, but he forfeited a 2007 Harley.

Still free, Peanut was ready to make more legitimate moves. He dabbled in funding films and getting into online porn, but it was in the hip-hop world that he experienced the most recognition. Someone introduced him to Philly rapper Charli Baltimore, who had once dated the Notorious B.I.G. Baltimore had been encouraged to rap by B.I.G., and Irv Gotti featured her on several Murder Inc. tracks but never released her album. Peanut and Baltimore hit it off and the two got together to launch BMB Records.

BMB Records started in 2013 in Detroit. It was an independent label with a stable of entertainers that, in addition to Baltimore, included R&B star Brandy's little brother Ray J; rapper Bre-Z, who starred on the hit Fox drama *Empire*; and rapper Kash Doll, a former exotic dancer, who signed with BMB after the label paid $15,000 for cosmetic surgery. BMB's music videos matched the label's flair, containing cinematic and dramatic cuts. Some featured Peanut himself.

Peanut Brown and his wife Akia established several other businesses as well as BMB Records, but the feds targeted the couple for years saying that the businesses were used to hide and disguise drug profits. The DEA claimed that the aspiring rap mogul was in fact one of the largest heroin dealers in the Midwest. They alleged that he reaped millions of dollars for almost a decade from the illicit business that he ran with a bunch of his homeboys.

The BMB label was registered to the same home that had been raided in 2012. Since then more than $1 million flowed into the label's two bank accounts between June 2013 and October 2015, and since January 2015 more than $350,00 was deposited through ATMs in Detroit and Baltimore. Investigators claimed Peanut's wife Akia was instrumental in his empire. She allegedly helped her husband hide assets and launder drug money.

The couple owned multiple homes in the metro Detroit area and a home near Atlanta. Akia Brown said she was a real estate agent, motivational speaker, and author. In 2009, however, a year before her husband finished his prison sentence, she was an unemployed mother of four with over $500,000 in debt and had filed bankruptcy. Now she was a self-described CEO with her own memoir, a billboard on the city's West Side, and a car collection valued at over $500,000—about fifteen times as much money as they reported on Peanut's 2011 taxes. The collection of twenty cars included a $94,000 Maserati, an $88,000 Cadillac Escalade, an $81,000 Porsche Panamera, plus two Corvettes.

Peanut Brown also had a business dispute with his artist Kash Doll (whose real name is Arkeisha Knight), who accused him of keeping a $5,000 signing bonus of hers and sued BMB Records with the help of Eminem's lawyer. Knight alleged that Brown coerced her into signing the recording agreement with BMB and said, "If you don't sign with me, I will destroy you and any career you think you have." She also claimed that Brown pursued her for his rap label because he liked "big boobs and butts."

Even with the fallout and lawsuit with BMB, the feds still raided Knight's home along with others suspected of being part of Peanut Brown's empire. DEA agents alleged that Brown was a hands-on leader of the drug ring and had arranged twice in 2014 to have money picked up and sent to another drug ring. Undercover DEA agents negotiated with Brown to pick up money at an Olive Garden restaurant. The agent received a black duffel bag filled with $240,000 in cash. Not knowing precisely where the money came from or the real reason why it was being delivered, the DEA agent could only assume, as he wrote in his files, that "he therefore believed that the $240,000 was from Brian Brown's proceeds of his drug trafficking operation."

Within months the investigation spread to California, but Brian "Peanut" Brown has not been charged with a drug crime despite an investigation that has lasted years. Peanut says he made his money legitimately. He has several legal businesses, and BMB Records is thriving. So far law enforcement apparently has nothing that can contradict the story that he emerged from a decade in prison and became a success in the hip-hop industry.

But the feds disagree and believe he's still a criminal. A fifty-page federal court record—written after he got out of prison in 2010—contradicts Brown's redemption story. "Any large-scale drug investigation inevitably takes many twists and turns along the way," Louis Gabel, a former assistant U.S. Attorney, told the *Detroit News*. "In many respects, it's like a choose-your-own-adventure book and each new page of the investigation presents new opportunities and challenges."

Once a featured fugitive on *America's Most Wanted*, Peanut Brown is now free. He's seemingly beaten the feds at their own game and appears untouchable, a street guy who has succeeded in the rap and entertainment world—pissing off investigators at every turn.

THE STORY OF THE SNITCHING STUDIO GANGSTER

BK

Tekashi 6ix9ine and the Nine Trey Gangsta Bloods

20

HIP-HOP CAME IN PART FROM A TRUCE between warring gangs. One drove the other. Gangs have always been present when it comes to hip-hop, and the two will be forever connected. So when you hear about gang culture now, know that it's nothing new. It's just cycling around. Most gangs formed to protect their neighborhoods and not do crime, but, as can happen, things get out of hand.

On the West Coast, the Crips gang formed, followed by the Bloods. This was in the late '60s, early '70s. The rise of violence from the two gangs surged in the '80s with the birth of the crack cocaine epidemic. The gangs then spread out and multiplied, relocating to other areas to expand their drug-dealing business. A kind of manifest destiny for gangs.

The culture of the Crips and Bloods reached the East Coast in the early '90s but was full blast in New York by 1995. The fastest city in the world now had so many sets of Bloods and Crips that it became a serious problem. And like their counterparts on the West Coast, they mixed hip-hop culture—its music and fashion—with gangbanging. It was a defiant statement to the powers that be—this is our culture.

Daniel Hernandez was born on May 28, 1996, in Bushwick, Brooklyn. His mother came from Mexico and his dad was Puerto Rican. Daniel also had a brother named Oscar who was two years older than he was. They were raised by both parents until their father left the family when Daniel was about nine. Daniel and Oscar were raised in the church, which they attended regularly. Daniel, who was called "Danny," played baseball and soccer throughout his youth.

Their mother later remarried. Both brothers were close with their step-father, who took good care of his new family. They were also doing well in school. In 2010 the stepfather was shot and killed steps away from the family's home. After their stepfather's murder, their mother didn't make enough money to support the family and couldn't pay the bills. She was forced to apply for welfare.

The brothers felt this struggle. They shared used clothes, and Danny had to share a bed with his mother. The death of his stepfather left Danny emotionally disturbed—he wasn't showering or eating and started losing weight. He needed therapy and was hospitalized for depression and post-traumatic stress disorder.

Danny started acting out in school and eventually got expelled. He ended up dropping out altogether. Instead of studying, he started working as a bagboy and delivery boy at a grocery store to help his mother with money. He first decided to rap in 2012 after meeting Peter "Righteous P" Rodgers, CEO of the New York label called Hikari-Ultra Records.

Danny was at work in a Bushwick deli when "Righteous P" saw him. He asked Danny if he could rap just based on Danny's appearance. He fit the image. This encounter gave Danny the energy to focus on becoming a rapper.

"Tekashi 6ix9ine" was born. He became known for his aggressive style of rapping, his controversial persona, his public feuds with celebrities, his rainbow-colored hair, and numerous tattoos—and, let's not ever forget, a pile of legal issues that turned him into a snitch.

Danny was placed in a rap group from the Brooklyn collective "Pro Era," with two other rappers, J.A.B. and Dirty Sanchez. Danny was the lead artist. They started releasing rap singles in 2014 starting with "69" in August 2014, "Pimpin" in September 2014, and two songs in October 2014 titled "Who the Fuck Is You" and "4769," which was featured with "Pro Era."

Now "69" spelled "6ix9ine" had a new label called FCK THEM based in Slovakia. He released multiple songs and videos such as "Scumlife." and "Hellsing Station." He became famous on the internet because of his bizarre appearance and aggressive rap style. He was also known as an associate of Righteous P's younger half-brother and fellow New York rapper ZillaKami, but they ended up feuding with each other, so 6ix9ine started working with a rapper named TrifeDrew, who he had collaborated with previously.

In October 2015, 6ix9ine was arrested after he had physical contact with a thirteen-year-old girl in a music video filmed in a trap house. He was sentenced to probation. Other arrests before that case involved an assault and a sale-of-heroin charge. At this time 6ix9ine was part of the Nine Trey Gangsta Bloods and shouted that out in songs and videos. He had inserted himself into gang culture at the same time his rap career was taking off.

6ix9ine worked on more songs. If anything, he was industrious. In April 2017 he released "Poles 1469" alongside Trippie Redd, and when they released the music video on YouTube, they released another song titled "Owee." Then, in July 2017, 6ix9ine rose to prominence on social media after an Instagram post went viral. His commercial debut single "Gummo" followed in November and peaked at number 12 on the Billboard 100 and went platinum. In the "Gummo" video, Tekashi bops around in pink and purple hair and a red bandana in front of several Nine Trey who flash gang signs. Danny from the deli would embrace this phony-thug image and use it to ride to the top.

He released the single "Kooda" and then in January 2018 released his third single, "KeKe," with rappers Fetty Wap and "A Boogie wit da Hoodie." 6ix9ine then released his debut mixtape, "Day69" in February. By 2018 6ix9ine was all over the internet and music charts as he released the songs "Gotti" and "FeFe." He was rocketing to stardom and his fellow Bloods were along for the ride.

"FeFe" featured Nicki Minaj and Murda Beatz and went double platinum. He then released the singles "Bebe" and "Stoopid." Even with all this success in music, 6ix9ine's name was not only known for his fame as a rapper—he was also known for being a member of the Nine Trey Gangsta Bloods (and for uttering the phrase "Treyway" in public). He was promoting his lifestyle and affiliation to the masses, and it was a significant part of his success.

"Mr. Hernandez only began rapping after he had achieved a taste of internet notoriety and he appeared to pursue gang life to bolster his musical endeavors," wrote journalists Ali Watkins and Joe Coscarelli in a *New York Times* profile. They observed, "For some rap stars, gang life was an unavoidable means of survival, and music offered a way out. For Mr. Hernandez, who also goes by the name Tekashi69, it was reversed: Gang affiliations lent authenticity to a rap career rooted more in sensationalism than in biography or in raw talent."

6ix9ine feuded with rappers in different camps, using drama to create notoriety. He clearly followed the strategy *of all publicity is good publicity* and beefed with several of Chicago's drill artists from the "Glo Gang" collective of rappers—Chief Keef, Lil Reese, and Tadoe. The feud with them took place in May 2018 when 6ix9ine was involved in a shooting with the entourage of fellow New York rapper Casanova as part of a yet another feud. This led to the rapper getting banned from the Barclays Center arena in Brooklyn and losing a $5 million headphone deal. You would think losing that deal would've woken him up but he was too far gone.

In July 2018, 6ix9ine was arrested in New York for an outstanding warrant connected to an incident in which he choked out a sixteen-year-old in a shopping mall in Houston. The charges were dropped. The previous month, on June 2, Chicago rapper Chief Keef was shot at outside the W Hotel in New York City because of an ongoing feud with 6ix9ine, who was later charged for ordering the attempted hit and pled guilty. 6ix9ine was making moves like he was a shot caller now, but in the gang's hierarchy money doesn't always equal power.

Following the incident, 6ix9ine was kidnapped, beaten, and robbed by three armed men in Brooklyn where he had just finished shooting the music video for "FeFe." The men grabbed him from outside his home, pistol-whipped him, and took $750,000 in custom jewelry and $40,000 in cash. 6ix9ine escaped by jumping out of their car and fleeing. It turned out that it was Nine Trey Gangsta members from his own camp who set him up, including Anthony "Harv" Ellison.

At his codefendants' 2019 trial 6ix9ine testified about Harv's role in the kidnapping and assault. Video footage from 6ix9ine's dash cam was played in court. "Don't shoot, don't shoot," 6ix9ine can be heard saying in the footage. "Everybody is saying, extortion this, extortion that . . . Harv, please, Harv, you know I'll give you everything, bro." 6ix9ine testified that he thought his assailants were going to kill him. They made him renounce his membership in the gang and extorted 6ix9ine for $750,000 worth of jewelry for sparing his life. Shit got real in a hurry for the rainbow-haired rapper.

The kid who called himself "Tekashi 6ix9ine" thought that his life was a movie in which he was the star, like a modern remake of *Colors*. At the same time he was being victimized and used as a pawn by his own gang.

To them he was a "mark." Nevertheless he started rap beefs that turned real and hid behind the Bloods. He thought the controversy would make him more famous and sell more units. He saw what controversy did for Curtis "50 Cent" Jackson. He wanted that kind of fame but wasn't prepared for the life that came with it.

This modern era of hip-hop requires that an artist really be about what they claim in their raps or else. That is the illusion being sold. *Fake it till you make it.* Tekashi 6ix9ine wanted to be known for the gangsta life he rapped about when in fact he was no gangster. He was ordering hits, not knowing his gang was only doing so to plunge him deeper into their trap. Gangbanging in lyrics and gangbanging in real life are two totally different things—look what happened to Tupac. Real gangsters don't broadcast their moves.

In November 2018, the feds arrested Daniel "Tekashi 6ix9ine" Hernandez on federal RICO charges, along with his former manager Kifano "Shotti" Jordan and three other associates. At one time Shotti had defended 6ix9ine and even beefed with Harv over him, but in the end Shotti was just trying to extort 6ix9ine for monetary gain. In a way Shotti played himself because it seems like he got caught up in being a music mogul—and, as the case of Suge Knight shows, it's risky to be a music mogul and a gangsta. Both occupations require different levels of game that don't always go together.

Hernandez was also charged with conspiracy to murder and armed robbery and faced up to life in prison. He was denied bail and kept in the federal detention center in general population, where he had multiple altercations with fellow prisoners, including members of the Crips street gang. If you are going to talk that gangsta shit you better be prepared to back it up at all times. Despite being in jail, 6ix9ine still had songs as well as features that hit the Billboard charts, such as "Swervin" on the album *Hoodie SZN* by A Boogie wit da Hoodie. He was still hot in music, as is said, and was about to become "hot" too in the parlance of prison (i.e., a snitch).

In February 2019, 6ix9ine pled guilty to nine charges and was scheduled to be sentenced in January 2020, facing a possible mandatory sentence of forty-seven years in prison. He avoided that sentence by becoming a snitch. He testified against fellow gang members in concurrent investigations. When the moment of truth came, 6ix9ine folded. He decided the *Death before Dishonor* code didn't apply to him.

On December 18, 2019, 6ix9ine was sentenced to two years after testifying against his codefendants and other Nine Trey Gangsta Blood members, including both Shotti and Harv, who got sentences of fifteen and twenty-four years, respectively, for their roles in the conspiracy. 6ix9ine was given credit by the judge for helping prosecutors send several violent gang members to prison and got thirteen months' time served.

He also snitched on other rappers. 6ix9ine claimed in court that rapper Trippie Redd was part of a rival crew called the Five-Nine Brims, which led to him being investigated. Hernandez also said Cardi B was part of Nine Trey and he saw her riding with some members, a claim she denies. What kind of gangsta is that? A cardboard one.

When court reports came out, the hip-hop world turned against 6ix9ine. There had often been claims that certain rappers like 50 Cent were snitches, but none so brazen in their snitching as 6ix9ine. Dry snitching in your raps and testifying in open court are two different things. Several rappers took to social media and the radio to aim venom at the face-tatted rat.

"The era I come from, you couldn't tell on a nigga, snitching, working with the federal government. After the government shutdown, the nigga decides to work with the federal government. I swear to god this new gangbanging shit is robotic to me," said West Coast O.G. Snoop Dogg on social media.

"Screw him. He did some actions that he can't come back from so his name, nonmentionable," said New York rapper Jim Jones in a radio interview. "I grew up in an era where certain things you cannot come back from. You a rat, you a rat forever. Ain't no coming back from that."

"If you're a fucking rat . . . you a rat . . . r-a-t. You get no respect," 21Savage said in an Instagram post.

In March 2020, Hernandez asked to serve the remainder of his prison sentence at home. He claimed he was at a higher risk of contracting the Covid-19 virus because he has asthma. He was granted the home confinement request and since his release, 6ix9ine has returned to the music industry. The song "Gooba" was released along with a music video. He also collaborated again with Nicki Minaj on a song titled "Trollz." "Yaya" and "Punani" were also singles released from last album *Tattle Tales*, released in September 2020.

Since getting out of prison, 6ix9ine has also engaged in several feuds with rap artists such as Future, YG, Rich the Kid, 50 Cent, Meek Mill, and others. He is back to starting controversy like this shit is a game. He even accused singers Ariana Grande and Justin Bieber of buying their way to number one on the Billboard Hot 100 and accused Billboard of chart manipulation. He also started beefing with rappers Lil Durk and Lil Reese and Lil Tjay. He was not taking this shit seriously like rappers don't get shot and killed too. In October 2020, 6ix9ine was hospitalized after he overdosed by combining Hydroxycut diet pills and coffee.

"He needs to go ahead and commit fucking suicide," said Nine Trey's ShaBoogie from the Bronx, who is wearing four life sentences in the feds for RICO charges similar to the charges 6ix9ine dodged. "Someone needs to kill him for all that faking he is doing in the hip-hop world and Bloods' movement. He got homies fucked up for life out there and in here. Shit ain't a game He's definitely food on the menu—shark food. Fucking SNITCH!"

Tekashi 6ix9ine continues to troll his enemies and dares them to chase him down. People who knew Hernandez well agree that, before he met Shotti, he hadn't been involved in gang life at all. Since his release a handful of highly publicized projects have come out that tell his story. The latest is Showtime's documentary series, *Supervillain: The Making of Tekashi 6ix9ine,* which followed Hulu's feature-length documentary *69: The Saga of Danny Hernandez.* Complex also did a podcast, *Infamous: The Tekashi 6ix9ine Story,* about the rapper turned snitch. As 2023 arrives 6ix9ine has faded from the scene. A splash turned ripple turned nothing.

Acknowledgments

Special thanks to my guy Shakim Bio, who is always ready to help and get the pulse of the prison landscape for me. Also, a big shout out to my guy Anthony Mathenia, who helped make this book possible with his tremendous feedback.

Sources

CHAPTER 1

Bio, Shakim. Personal interview, July 7, 2021.

Bogazianos, Dimitri. *5 Grams: Crack Cocaine, Rap Music, and the War on Drugs*. New York: New York University Press, 2012.

Hands, Dan. Personal interview, August 6, 2021.

"Lil D on Becoming Crack King, Getting 35 Years, Obama Clemency (full interview)." VladTV. https://youtu.be/Hc9kOILif54

McDuffie, Damien. "Torn Apart by Reagan, One Family Gets a Second Chance from Obama." *Complex*, November 1, 2016.

CHAPTER 2

Kenner, Rob. "Interview: J. Prince Talks About the Rise of Rap-A-Lot Records." *Complex*, December 4, 2011. https://www.complex.com/music/2011/12/interview-j-prince-talks-about-the-rise-of-rap-a-lot-records

Noz, Andrew. "'It Was Like Flies to Honey': 25 Years of Rap-A-Lot Records." The Record Music News from NPR, February 10, 2012. https://www.npr.org/sections/therecord/2012/01/23/143799814/it-was-like-flies-to-honey-25-years-of-rap-a-lot-records

Prince, James. *The Art and Science of Respect: A Memoir by James Prince*. Houston: N-The-Water Publishing, 2018.

Rogan, Joe. "#1581—J Prince." *The Joe Rogan Experience*, December 18, 2020. https://www.jrepodcast.com/episode/joe-rogan-experience-1581-j-prince/

CHAPTER 3

Andrich, Frank. "N.W.A. Interview." *Shark* (Germany), June 1989.

Fab 5 Freddy. Interview with N.W.A. *Yo! MTV Raps*. 1991.

Harrington, Richard. "The FBI as Music Critic." *Washington Post*, October 4, 1989.

Hiatt, Brian. "Hear Ice Cube Reveal N.W.A.'s Secret History." *Rolling Stone*, August 29, 2018.

Kennedy, Gerrick. *Parental Discretion Is Advised: The Rise of N.W.A. and the Dawn of Gangsta Rap*. New York: Atria, 2018.

McCann, Bryan J. *The Mark of Criminality: Rhetoric, Race, and Gangsta Rap in the War-on-Crime Era*. Tuscaloosa, AL: University of Alabama Press, 2017.

Owen, Frank. "N.W.A. Hanging Tough." *SPIN*, April 1990.

Savidge, S. Leigh. *Welcome to Death Row: The Uncensored History of the Rise and Fall of Death Row Records in the Words of Those Who Were There*. Santa Monica, CA: Xenon Press, 2015.

Viator, Felicia Angeja. *To Live and Defy in LA: How Gangsta Rap Changed America*. Cambridge: Harvard University Press, 2020.

CHAPTER 4

Jacobs, Emily. "Death Row Records Co-founder Michael 'Harry-O' Harris Thanks Trump for Pardon." *New York Post*, January 27, 2021.

Reavill, Gil, and Jerry Heller. *Ruthless: A Memoir*. New York: Simon & Schuster, 2007.

Savidge, S. Leigh. *Welcome to Death Row: The Uncensored History of the Rise and Fall of Death Row Records in the Words of Those Who Were There*. Santa Monica, CA: Xenon Press, 2015.

Westhoff, Ben. *Original Gangstas: Tupac Shakur, Dr. Dre, Eazy-E, Ice Cube, and the Birth of West Coast Rap*. New York: Hatchette Book Group, 2017.

CHAPTER 5

Atkins, Jermaine. *Zoe Pound Mafia: The Haitians That Took Over the Streets and Muscled the Hip-Hop Industry*. BOATS Publishing, 2016.

Campbell, Luther. *The Book of Luke: My Fight for Truth, Justice, and Liberty City*. New York: HarperCollins, 2015.

Chiles, Tiffany. "The Real History of Miami's Zoe Pound." *Don Diva Magazine*, #37, January 1, 2009.

"Jim Jones Tells Story of Ali 'Zoe' Adam and Zoe Pound Being First to Make It Rain in Clubs." The Official Zoe Pound. https://www.youtube.com/watch?v=lgzfNIQOel8

Whiteside, Regan, and Ali Adam. *The HIP-HOP B.L.A.C.K. Republican Party Manifest.* CreateSpace Publishing, 2018.

CHAPTER 6

Alvarez, Aida. "Savage Skulls Feared as Worst Bronx Gang," *New York Post*, September 15, 1975.

Bilmes, Alex. "Jay-Z on His Music, Politics, and His Violent Past." *GQ*, June 28, 2017.

"Calvin Klein Bacote on Getting Arrested with Jay-Z." VladTV. https://www.youtube.com/watch?v=3OI1B_5q93Y

Chang, Jeff. *Can't Stop Won't Stop: A History of the Hip-Hop Generation.* New York: St. Martin's Press, 2007.

Cooper, Mark. "NWA: 'Our Raps Are Documentary. We Don't Take Sides.'" *The Guardian*, August 7, 2013.

Davey D. "Interview w/ DJ Kool Herc, 1989 New Music Seminar." https://www.daveyd.com/interviewkoolherc89.html

Jay-Z. *Decoded.* New York: Random House, 2011.

Perry, Imani. *Prophets of the Hood: Politics and Poetics in Hip Hop.* Durham, NC: Duke University Press, 2004.

Quinn, Eithne. *Nuthin' but a "G" Thang: The Culture and Commerce of Gangsta Rap.* New York: Columbia University Press, 2005.

Robison, Lisa. "Jay Z Has the Room," *Vanity Fair*, October 14, 2013.

CHAPTER 7

Harmanci, Reyhan and Shoshana Walter. "Federal Drug Case Ensnares the Home of Hyphy." The Record—Music News from NPR, September 9, 2013.

"J-Diggs on Mac Dre, Bank Robberies, Prison, Messy Marv Beef (full interview)." VladTV. https://youtu.be/h-JCzX-cMRw

The Legend of the Bay. Dir. Zachary Butler, Andre Louis Entertainment, 2015.

"Pizza Restaurant Robbers." *Unsolved Mysteries.* 1992

Shakim Bio. Personal interview, July 7, 2021.

"Too $hort on His Music & Women, Longevity in the Game, New Generation & More." DJ Scream, *Big Facts.* https://www.youtube.com/watch?v=wFZNUa2Z1gc

"Vallejo-Based Rappers Arrested as Part of Major Investigation of Drug Trafficking Throughout the United States." U.S. Attorney's Office, Eastern District of California, FBI Press Release, April 24, 2012.

CHAPTER 8

"Ayanna Jackson on Meeting 2Pac, Sexual Assault, Trial, Aftermath (full interview)." VladTV. https://www.youtube.com/watch?v=0CVBOv9O1GA

Brown, Ethan. *Queens Reigns Supreme: Fat Cat, 50 Cent, and the Rise of the Hip Hop Hustler*. New York: Anchor Books, 2010.

Chiles, Tiffany. "Who is Jimmy Henchman?" *Don Diva Magazine*, #55, January 1, 2014.

Hova, Tray. "BREAKING: Jimmy Henchman Affiliate Admits to Shooting Tupac; Apologizes." *Vibe*, June 15, 2011.

"Jimmy Henchmen Interview." Blowhiphoptv.com. https://www.youtube.com/watch?v=LWeL1Q738oU

"'UNJUST' Free James Rosemond aka Jimmy Henchman." The Official Zoe Pound. https://www.youtube.com/watch?v=dZrNVxPxM-c

"Unjust Justice: The James Rosemond Story," Hosted by Michael K. Williams. *Criminal Minded Media Podcast*. March 21, 2022.

Watkins, Grouchy. "EXCLUSIVE: James 'Jimmy Henchman' Rosemond Sentenced to Life; Official Statement." AllHipHop, October 25, 2013. https://allhiphop.com/headlines/exclusive-james-jimmy-henchman-rosemond-sentenced-to-life-official-statement

CHAPTER 9

Chiles, Kevin. *The Crack Era: The Rise, Fall and Redemption of Kevin Chiles*. New York: DDMG, 2019.

Chiles, Tiffany. "New Jack City's Last Man Standing: The Kevin Chiles Story," *Don Diva*, #9, January 1, 2004.

Ferranti, Seth. "Kevin Chiles: Penthouse Interview." *Penthouse*, November 18, 2019.

"FULL CAVARIO: Ex Kingpin, Businessman & Author Issues with Gully TV & 50 Cent, Don Diva, Prison Reform & More." Big Face Gary Show. https://youtu.be/nd19kwr-oVU

"Kevin Chiles on His Rise and Fall as a Harlem Drug Kingpin (full interview)." DJ Vlad, VladTV. https://youtu.be/P2nTu6ddkoE

CHAPTER 10

"A-Man." Personal interview, August 16, 2021.

Noel, Peter. "Big Bad Wolf." *The Village Voice*, February 13, 2001.

Shakim Bio. Personal interview, July 14, 2021.

CHAPTER 11

Campbell, Luther. *The Book of Luke: My Fight for Truth, Justice, and Liberty City.* New York: HarperCollins, 2015.

Chiles, Tiffany, "Miami's The Boobie Boys: 35 Murders & 100 Shootings." *Don Diva Magazine*, #41, January 1, 2010.

"Convertible Burt on Crack Hitting Miami, Making Millions, Doing 25 Years (full interview)." VladTV. https://youtu.be/crtRPN7ASl8

Ross, Rick with Neil Martinez-Belkin. *Hurricanes: A Memoir.* New York: Hanover Square Press, 2019.

"Ted Lucas Divulges Keys to Slip-N-Slide Records' 20-Year Run." Hip HopDX. https://hiphopdx.com/interviews/id.2305/title.ted-lucas-divulges -keys-to-slip-n-slide-records-20-year-run

Trapital. "Ted Lucas on Slip-N-Slide Records, Miami Hip-Hop, and R&B's Comeback | Trapital Podcast Interview." Trapital. https:// youtu.be/2wOmmQIZG-4

CHAPTER 12

"Birdman Clears Up Cash Money Records Rumors, Past Issues with Charlamagne, Rick Ross, & More." DJ Scream, *Big Facts.* https:// youtu.be/kZMLzh_E2PI

"Birdman's Brother Terrance 'Gangsta' Williams Tells His Life Story (full interview)." DJ Vlad, VladTV. https://www.youtube.com/watch? v=LQ7eZ5XHgL0

"Boosie on NBA YoungBoy, Terrance 'Gangsta' Williams, Yung Bleu, R Kelly, Lis Nas X (full interview)." DJ Vlad, VladTV. https://youtu.be/ mq-t7zw4WKA

Dougherty, Terri. *The Story of Cash Money Records.* Broomall, PA: Mason Crest, 2014.

"4 Sync Up Keynote Interview: Slim Williams of Cash Money Records." New Orleans Jazz & Heritage Foundation. https://youtu.be/I57isbEis-U

CHAPTER 13

"Bimmy on Supreme Team, 50 Cent, Bobby Brown, Waka Flocka, Jam Master Jay (full interview)." DJ Vlad, VladTV. https://www.youtube.com /watch?v=XiR4GeL8_8w

"Irv Gotti on 'Tales,' 50 Cent Beef, Beating Fed Case, Nas, Jay Z, Suge Knight (full interview)." DJ Vlad, VladTV. https://youtu.be/zUdInoRAzpU

Parker, Derrick, and Matt Diehl. *Notorious C.O.P.: The Inside Story of the Tupac, Biggie, and Jam Master Jay Investigations from NYPD's First "Hip-Hop Cop."* New York: St. Martin's Press, 2007.

Shakim Bio. Personal interview, July 14, 2021.

CHAPTER 14

"Dee of Ruff Ryders on Getting Involved in Streets While Being Raised a Muslim." DJ Vlad, VladTV. https://youtu.be/2H3YO3msgN0

Fontaine, Smokey D. *E.A.R.L.: The Autobiography of DMX.* New York: HarperCollins, 2003.

Reynolds, Simon. *Bring the Noise: 20 Years of Writing About Hip Rock and Hip Hop.* New York: Soft Skull Press, 2011.

"Waah Dean on Starting Ruff Ryders, Signing DMX." DJ Vlad, VladTV. https://youtu.be/0iUepIJZ8ck

CHAPTER 15

"Ace Capone Story: Live from Federal Prison (Philly FAME Flashback)." Philly F.A.M.E. https://youtu.be/l0dDun4byYg

Anastasia, George, "The Takedown of Ace Capone," *The Inquirer*, November 11, 2007.

Capone, A. T. *Go Hard: The Takedown of Ace Capone.* Createspace Independent Publishing, 2012.

Shakim Bio. Personal interview, August 4, 2021.

Watkins, Greg. "Philly Drug Kingpin Ace Capone Releases Tell-All, 'Go Hard: The Takedown of Ace Capone,'" AllHipHop, August 30, 2012. https://allhiphop.com/mobile/philly-drug-kingpin-ace-capone-releases -tell-all-go-hard-the-takedown-of-ace-caponea/

CHAPTER 16

"Lupe Fiasco on Jay-Z Offering Him a Deal at Rock-A-Fella Records (Chapter 5)." The Coda Collection. https://youtu.be/688TxwDKWZM

"Lupe Fiasco Producer Sentenced to 44 Years." *The St. Louis American*, June 4, 2007.

"Lupe Fiasco's Business Partner Sentenced to 44 Years for Drug Charges." *Baller Status*, June 4, 2007. https://www.ballerstatus.com/2007/06/04 /lupe-fiascos-business-partner-sentenced-to-44-years-for-drug-charges/

"Rapper Lupe Fiasco Accused of Hiding Money for a Drug Kingpin," *TMZ*, September 3, 2013. https://www.tmz.com/2013/09/03/rapper-lupe-fiasco -charles-patton-drug-divorce-hiding-money/

CHAPTER 17

Mane, Gucci, with Neil Martinez-Belkin. *The Autobiography of Gucci Mane*. New York: Simon & Schuster, 2017.

Rahim/"Fly Paul." Personal interview, August 17, 2021.

Shalhoup, Mara. *BMF: The Rise and Fall of Big Meech and the Black Mafia Family*. New York: St. Martin's Press, 2010.

Shalhoup, Mara. "BMF—Hip-Hop's Shadowy Empire, Part 3." Creative Loafing, December 20, 2006. https://creativeloafing.com /content-196221-bmf—hip-hop-s-shadowy-empire—part

Vance, JJ. *Gucci Mane Book—A Biography of Greatness: The Life and Times of Gucci Mane Legendary Hip-Hop Trap Rapper: Gucci Mane Book for Our Generation*. J. J. Vance, 2021.

CHAPTER 18

Diaz, Angel. "Exclusive: Bobby Shmurda and Rowdy Rebel Give First Interview Since Plea Deal." *Complex*, September 15, 2016.

Lilah, Rose. "Bobby Shmurda & GS9 Arrest by the Numbers," *HotNewHipHop*, December 19, 2014. https://www.hotnewhiphop .com/29263-bobby-shmurda-and-gs9-arrest-by-the-numbers-news

Johnson, Albert "Prodigy," and Laura Checkoway. *My Infamous Life: The Autobiography of Mobb Deep's Prodigy*. New York: Touchstone Books, 2011.

Pegues, Corey. *Once a Cop: The Street, the Law, Two Worlds, One Man*. New York: Atria Publishing Group, 2017.

Shakim Bio. Personal interview, August 18, 2021.

Smith, Ryan. "P Gutta of GS9 Speaks on Beef with 50 Cent, The Bobby Shmurda Trial, and More." *Don Diva Magazine*, January 1, 2016

CHAPTER 19

Davenport, Treavion. *Living for the Sacrifice a Hood Hero's Guide to Success*. New York: BMB Publishing, 2017.

"Kash Doll on Dancing, Drake, Big Sean, Dex Osama Getting Killed, Music (full interview)." DJ Vlad, VladTV. https://youtu.be/lEYZjB7DnyI

Sincere. Personal interview, September 3, 2021.

Snell, Robert. "Detroit Empire: Feds Say Rap Mogul Is Heroin Kingpin." *Detroit News*, March 29, 2017.

CHAPTER 20

Guerrero, Melissa. "Tekashi 69: How His Trial Left Him Labeled a 'Snitch.'" *New York Times*, May 20, 2020.

"Infamous: The Tekashi 6ix9ine Story." *Complex Podcast,* January 23, 2020. https://www.complex.com/podcasts/tekashi-6ix-9ine-podcast

About the Author

AFTER LANDING ON THE U.S. MARSHALS SERVICE "15 Most Wanted" list and being sentenced to a twenty-five-year sentence in federal prison for a first-time, nonviolent LSD and cannabis offense, Seth Ferranti built a writing and journalism career from his cell block in the "belly of the beast." His raw portrayals of prison life and crack-era gangsters have appeared in *Don Diva*, *VICE*, and *Penthouse*. From prison Ferranti published books like *Prison Stories* and *Street Legends*, which made him a celebrity in and out of penitentiaries across the United States and abroad. His incredible story has been covered by the *Washington Post*, the *Washington Times*, *High Times*, and *Rolling Stone,* and he starred in the Season 1 finale of VICE's *I Was A Teenage Felon*. He wrote, produced, and appeared in the hit Netflix documentary *White Boy* and will have released three feature documentaries—*Nightlife*, *Dopemen*, and *A Tortured Mind*—by the time this book is published.

Thug Life is set in 10-point Sabon, which was designed by the German-born typographer and designer Jan Tschichold (1902–1974) in the period 1964–1967. It was released jointly by the Linotype, Monotype, and Stempel type foundries in 1967. Copyeditor for this project was Shannon LeMay-Finn. The book was designed by Brad Norr Design, Minneapolis, Minnesota, and typeset by New Best-set Typesetters Ltd.